L. W. (Lazarus Whitehead) Powell

Military Interference with Elections

Speech of Hon. L.W. Powell, of Kentucky, delivered in the Senate of the

United States, March 3 and 4, 1864

L. W. (Lazarus Whitehead) Powell

Military Interference with Elections
Speech of Hon. L.W. Powell, of Kentucky, delivered in the Senate of the United States, March 3 and 4, 1864

ISBN/EAN: 9783337153731

Printed in Europe, USA, Canada, Australia, Japan

Cover: Foto ©ninafisch / pixelio.de

More available books at **www.hansebooks.com**

SPEECH

OF

ON. L. W. POWELL,

OF KENTUCKY,

,IVERED IN THE SENATE OF THE UNITED STATES,

MARCH 3 AND 4, 1864.

ON

BILL TO PREVENT OFFICERS OF THE ARMY AND NAVY, AND OTHER PERSONS ENGAGED IN THE MILITARY AND NAVAL SERVICE OF THE UNITED STATES, FROM INTERFERING IN ELECTIONS IN THE STATES.

WASHINGTON, D. C.:
PRINTED AT CONSTITUTIONAL UNION OFFICE.
1864.

SPEECH.

The Senate, as in Committee of the Whole, proceeded to consider the bill (S. No. 37) to prevent officers of the army and navy, and other persons engaged in the military and naval service of the United States, from interfering in elections in the States.

The bill was read by the Secretary. The first section provides that it shall not be lawful for any military or naval officer of the United States, or other person engaged in the civil, military, or naval service of the United States, to order, bring, keep, or have under his authority or control, any troops or armed men within one mile of the place where any general or special election is held in any State of the United States of America, and that it shall not be lawful for any officer of the army or navy of the United States to prescribe or fix, or attempt to prescribe or fix, by proclamation, order, or otherwise, the qualifications of voters in any State, or in any manner to interfere with the freedom of any election, or with the exercise of the free right of suffrage in any State. Any officer of the army or navy, or other person engaged in the civil, military, or naval service of the United States who violates this section is for every such offense to be liable to indictment as for a misdemeanor,.in any court of the United States having jurisdiction to hear, try, and determine cases of misdemeanor, and on conviction to pay a fine of not less than $200, and not exceeding $20,000, and suffer imprisonment in the penitentiary not less than two nor more than twenty years, at the discretion of the court; and any person so convicted is moreover to be disqualified from holding any office of honor, profit, or trust, under the Government of the United States. The bill is not, however, to be so construed as to prevent any officer, soldier, sailor, or marine, from exercising the right of suffrage in any election district to which he may belong, if otherwise qualified, according to the laws of the State in which he shall offer to vote.

By the second section any officer or person in the military or naval service of the United States, who shall order or advise, or who shall directly or indirectly, by force, threat, menace, intimidation or otherwise, prevent or attempt to prevent any qualified voter of any State from freely exercising the right of suffrage at any general or special election, or who shall in like manner compel or attempt to compel, any officer of an election in any State to receive a vote from a person not legally qualified to vote, or who shall impose or attempt to impose any rules or regulations for conducting such election different from those prescribed by law, or interfere in any manner with any officer of the election in the discharge of his duties, is for any such offense to be liable. to indictment as for misdemeanor, in any court of the United States having jurisdiction to hear, try, and determine cases of misdemeanor, and on conviction to pay a fine not exceeding $20,000, and suffer imprisonment in the penitentiary, not exceeding five years, at the discretion of the court, and any person so convicted is moreover to be disqualified from holding any office of honor, profit, or trust, under the Government of the United States.

Mr. POWELL said:

Mr. PRESIDENT: The object of the bill is to prevent officers of the army and navy, and other persons engaged in the military and naval service of the United States,. from intering with elections in the States. The bill provides that the persons named, if they interfere with elections in the States, shall be punished, upon trial and conviction in the courts, by fine and imprisonment, and shall be forever after disqualified from holding any office of honor, trust or profit, under the Government of the United States. The importance of the bill at the present crisis in our affairs cannot be over-estimated. In times of profound peace and quiet, when no abuses of the character proposed to be remedied by this bill existed, it would. be evidently wise and proper to enact such a law. Wise lawgivers so shape their legislation as to prevent as far as possible all abuses that are calculated to sap the foundations of the political system, to impair or destroy the fundamental law, or to endanger or overthrow the rights or liberties of the people.

It cannot be doubted that upon the keeping of the elective franchise absolutely free depends the very existence of our form of Government and our republican institutions. Free States in all ages have regarded the purity of the elective franchise as of the greatest and most vital importance, and have enacted severe penal laws for the punishment of those who interfered by force or fraud to prevent free elections. I believe there is no Government on the face of the earth in which elections have been carried on for the purpose of appointing any of the officers of the Government, save and except the United States of America, that has not had laws to punish, and severely punish those who should interfere with the freedom of the elective franchise. All the republics of antiquity had the severest laws punishing those who interfered with the freedom of their elections. In the second volume of Blackstone's Commentaries, by Mr. Tucker, on page 170, I find this :

"For in a democracy there can be no exercise of sovereignty but by suffrage, which is the declaration of the people's will. In all democracies, therefore, it is of the utmost importance to regulate by whom, and in what manner, the suffrages are to be given. And the Athenians were so justly jealous of this prerogative, that a stranger who interfered in the assemblies of the people was punished by their laws with death ; because such a man was esteemed guilty of high treason by usurping those rights of sovereignty to which he had no title. In England, where the people do not debate in a collective body but by representation, the exercise of this sovereignty consists in the choice of representatives. The laws have therefore been strictly guarded against usurpation or abuse of this power by many salutary provisions, which may be reduced to these three points : 1. The qualifications of the electors. 2. The qualifications of the elected. 3. The proceedings at elections."

By the laws of Great Britain persons convicted of bribery, force, or fraud at elections are punished severely. At the common law, bribery and kindred offenses were crimes, and the British statutes punished persons guilty of such offenses on conviction with fines of £500, and deprived them of the privilege ever after of voting or holding any office of trust or honor under that government. One section of this bill provides that the soldiers of the army of the United States shall not be permitted to be kept within one mile of any poll where an election is going on, on the day of election. I find similar provisions in the English law, which I will read from page 179 of the same book :

"As soon, therefore, as the time and place of election, either in counties or boroughs, are fixed, all soldiers quartered in the place are to remove, at leas t one day before the election, to the distance of two miles or more, and not to return till one day after the poll is ended. Riots, likewise, have been frequently determined to make an election void."

By a statute passed in the reign of George II, to which I alluded in a running debate that arose upon the reference of this bill to a committee, and which statute is quoted at length in the report made by the Committee on Military Affairs, it is provided that the Secretary of War,

or the party who for the time being is acting as Secretary of War, shall issue his orders to remove all soldiers from places of voting in the manner prescribed in the law I have just read. It further provides that if the Secretary of War or the person acting as such shall not issue the order as required by the statute, he shall upon conviction in the courts be dismissed from office, and be ever after disqualified from holding any office of honor, profit, or trust, under the British Government.

That is the manner in which our English ancestors, from whom we have derived most of our maxims of civil and constitutional liberty, regarded this subject. Mr. Tucker, in his notes to Blackstone's Commentaries, in reference to the law I have read requiring soldiers to be removed from the place of voting, says, "A similar regulation in the election of Representatives to Congress seems highly proper and necessary." It is strange to me that we have never had such a law on our statute-book. I venture the assertion that we are the only. people on earth who have had any regard for free government that have not had some such law. I suppose the only reason for the absence of such a law is that our elections have been regulated heretofore by officers appointed by the States, and it is only very recently that the armies of the United States have attempted to interfere in our elections.

By the spirit of the Constitution of the United States, and by the constitution of every State in the Union, the military is to be kept in strict subordination to the civil power; and I suppose that those who went before us never thought we should have rulers so wicked and corrupt as to use the machinery of the Federal Government for the purpose of prostrating the freedom of elections in the States : otherwise, I am sure that such laws as the one before us would have been enacted long before this. I find upon examination that seven of the States of the Union have enacted statutes to prevent soldiers making their appearance on election day at the places where the elections are held. I shall not trouble the Senate by reading all these statutes ; but as the State of Maryland—unfortunately for the honor and dignity of that State—figures a good deal in this matter, I will take the liberty of reading the statutes of Maryland from her Code, volume I, page 262 :

"Article 35—Elections.

"SEC. 24. No commissioned or non-commissioned officer having the command of any soldier or soldiers quartered or posted in any district of any county in this State shall muster or embody any of the said troops, or march any recruiting party within the view of any place of election during the time of holding said election, under the penalty of $100. This section not to apply to the city of Baltimore."

I have similar provisions here from the statutes of the State of Mississippi, New Jersey, New York, Pennsylvania, Maine, and Massachusetts. The constitution of the State of Maryland provides that upon conviction for the offense of giving or receiving bribes or influencing any man to give an illegal vote, not only the man giving the bribe but the man giving the illegal vote shall forever after be disqualified from voting and from holding any office of trust, honor, or profit under the State government. Every State in the Union has severe penal laws, providing for the punishment of all who in any way interfere to prevent free elections.

With us, Mr. President, sovereignty resides in the people, and the people by the exercise of free suffrage declare their will and appoint their agencies to carry on the Government. He who attempts to interfere with this most inestimable right, whether he be President, major-general, or citizen, is an enemy to the Republic and deserves the harshest punishment. In order to have free elections, there must be free speech and a free press; the sovereign people must have an opportunity of forming an enlightened public opinion upon the questions at issue, which can only be done after full and free discussion. Free speech and a free press in a Government like ours are the soul of republican institutions; free suffrage is the very heart-strings of civil liberty. To be free, the elections must be conducted in accordance with laws so framed as to prevent fraud, force, intimidation, corruption, and venality, superintended by election judges and officers independent of the Executive or any other power of the Government; the military must not interfere, but be kept in strict subordination to the law which should be so framed as to prevent absolutely such interference. The only duty of the Executive is to see that the law is faithfully executed. The Executive must not use the power intrusted to him to prevent free elections. Mr. Locke, in his excellent treatise on Government, page 379, speaking of the executive power, says:

"What I have said here concerning the legislative in general, holds true also concerning the supreme executor, who having a double trust put in him, both to have a part in the legislative and the supreme execution of the law, acts against both when he goes about to set up his own arbitrary will as the law of society. He acts also contrary to his trust when he either employs the force, treasure, and offices of the society to corrupt the representatives and gain them to his purpose, or openly pre-engage the electors and prescribes to their choice such whom he has by solicitations, threats, promises, or otherwise won to his designs, and employs them to bring in such who have promised beforehand what to vote and what to enact. Thus to regulate candidates and electors and new-model the ways of election, what is it but to cut up the Government by the roots and poison the very fountain of public security? for the people have reserved to themselves the choice of their representatives, as the fence of their properties, could do it for no other end but that they might always be freely chosen, and, so chosen freely act and advise as the necessity of the Commonwealth and the public good should upon examination and mature debate be judged to require. This, those who give their votes before they hear the debate and have weighed the reasons on all sides are not capable of doing. To prepare such an assembly as this, and endeavor to set up the declared abettors of his own will for the true representatives of the people and the law-makers of the society, is certainly as great a breach of trust and as perfect a declaration of a design to subvert the Government as is possible to be met with."

Nothing can be truer than the sentiment uttered by Mr. Locke in the extract I have just read. It is certainly a subversion of the very foundation of the Government for the Executive to use the force and the power that the Government has placed in his hands for defensive purposes, to overthrow the free suffrages of the people and to appoint those to power who will be his truckling menials, his subservient agents to carry out his will, to aid him it may be to overthrow the liberties of the people whom they should represent, betray the Constitution that they should preserve and protect, destroy everything that makes the Government desirable and worthy of the support of an honest and free people. Yet, sir, such things have been done, and I regret to say that there are those in the Senate Chamber who not only do not denounce but who approve these usurpations, these plain, palpable violations of the Constitution of their country.

Mr. President, let us for a moment see what are the powers of the President of the United States. From whence does he derive this power to regulate elections and to appoint representatives of the people? for when stripped of its verbiage that is really what has been done in many parts of the States of Maryland, Missouri, Kentucky, and Delaware. Where, I ask, does the Executive of the United States derive such power? He certainly does not derive it from the Constitution. The second and third section of the second article of the Constitution prescribes the duties of the President. Let us read those clauses of the Constitution and see what powers are conferred upon the Chief Magistrate. I hold that the President can exercise no power but what is conferred upon him by the Constitution. He is the agent of the people appointed for specific purposes to administer their Government as its Executive, within prescribed and limited powers. The Constitution provides, in article two:

"SEC. 2. The President shall be Commander-in-Chief of the Army and Navy of the United States, and of the militia of the several States, when called into the actual service of the United States; he may require the opinion in writing of the principal officer in each of the Executive Departments upon any subject relating to the duties of their respective offices, and he shall have power to grant reprieves and pardons for offenses against the United States, except in cases of impeachment.

"He shall have power, by and with the advice and consent of the Senate, to make treaties, provided two-thirds of the Senators present concur; and he shall nominate, and, by and with the advice and consent of the Senate, shall appoint embassadors, other public ministers and consuls, judges of the Supreme Court, and all other officers of the United States whose appointments are not herein otherwise provided for, and which shall be established by law; but the Congress may by law vest the appointment of such inferior officers as they think proper in the President alone, in the courts of law, or in the heads of Departments.

"The President shall have power to fill up all vacancies that may happen during the recess of the Senate by granting commissions which shall expire at the end of their next session.

"SEC. 3. He shall from time to time give to the Congress information of the state of the Union, and recommend to their consideration such measures as he shall judge necessary and expedient; he may, on extraordinary occasions, convene both Houses, or either of them; and in case of disagreement between them with respect to the time of adjournment, he may adjourn them to such time as he shall think proper; he shall receive embassadors and other public ministers; he shall take care that the laws be faithfully executed, and shall commission all the officers of the United States."

There, sir, are the powers of the President of the United States. He is Commander-in-Chief of the armies of the United States, and under that clause I suppose those who oppose the bill claim that the President can rightfully exercise the power that he has exercised in overthrowing the freedom of elections in Maryland and other States. They claim it under the war power, which I will notice in another part of my remarks. The President is to "take care that the laws be faithfully executed." What laws are they that the President shall see faithfully executed? The Constitution declares that—

"This Constitution and the laws of the United States which shall be made in pursuance thereof, and all treaties made or which shall be made under the authority of the United States, shall be the supreme law of the land."

These are the laws that the President is to see faithfully executed. Whenever he goes beyond that he is a usurper. The President, under the Constitution, can exercise no implied power. All the implied powers that can be exercised under our Government must be exercised by another and a different body of magistracy, to wit, the legislative; and that is the express language of the Constitution. The eighteenth paragraph of the eighth section of the first article of the Constitution declares that Congress is clothed with the power to make all laws which shall be necessary and proper for carrying into effect all the powers vested by the Constitution in the Government of the United States, or in any Department or officer thereof; consequently the President can exercise no implied powers. He can exercise no power except that with which he is clothed by the Constitution and the laws made in pursuance thereof.

In the States to which I have alluded, the President, or those acting under his orders, have prescribed the qualifications of voters and the qualifications of candidates for office, and that, too, in direct violation of the Constitution of the United States. This is a grave charge, but it is one that I will make good by testimony that none can doubt. Let us see who it is that has the right to prescribe the qualifications of voters. I suppose that no Senator will deny that as to all State offices the States have the power to prescribe the qualifications of the officer as well as of the voter. That power not having been delegated by the Constitution to the General Government, the States necessarily retain it. But there is an express provision of the Constitution—the tenth amendment—which declares, "The powers not delegated to the United States by the Constitution, nor prohibited by it to the States, are reserved to the States respectively or to the people," and the Constitution very clearly indicates who are qualified voters for members of Congress. The second section of the first article of the Constitution is in these words:

"The House of Representatives shall be composed of members chosen every second year by the people of the several States, and the electors in each State shall have the qualifications requisite for electors of the most numerous branch of the State Legislature."

The Constitution of the United States, in the clause just read, declares who shall be qualified electors for members of Congress. It fixes the qualification as the one ordained by the State government for the members of the most numerous branch of their Legislature. That is the fundamental law of the land; but in violation of that provision of the Constitution the military have seen fit, by military orders, to fix the qualifications of voters in the States. They have gone further, and fixed the qualifications for office. Not only the military have done this, but the President of the United States himself has done it. I am not going to waste all my time upon those who do the Chief Magistrate's bidding, but it is my purpose to-day to expose his atrocious violations of the Constitution. I trust that I shall speak of the President in a manner that is courteous, but I certainly shall do it in very plain language. The charges that I have to make I trust will not be misunderstood by any one. I will not deal in inuendo, insinuation, or hint, but I will make the charge directly, and I have the proof to sustain it.

The second section of the first article of the Constitution fixes the qualifications of a Representative in Congress:

"No person shall be a Representative who shall not have attained to the age of twenty-five years, and been seven years a citizen of the United States, and who shall not, when elected, be an inhabitant of that State in which he shall be chosen."

The Committee on Military Affairs, who made a very elaborate report, which I have before me, and which I shall presently review, justify the military in all they have done in controlling elections. The sole object and design of the committee in their report seems to be the justification and vindication of the military authorities for their atrocious assault on the rights of the States and the liberties of the people and their wicked and illegal interference in elections; and they assault every person who says or does anything tending to prove that the military have usurped powers that belong to the civil officers of the States and to the people. The committee justify the President and the military authorities for this interference in elections upon the ground that it was right and proper that the military arm should have been so used to protect the voters, "the loyal voters," as they are called in the report. The Constitution prescribes the duty of the Chief Magistrate on this subject. I will read the clause from article four:

"Sec. 4. The United States shall guaranty to every State in this Union a republican form of government, and shall protect each of them against invasion, and, on application of the Legislature, or of the Executive, (when the Legislature cannot be convened,) against domestic violence."

The President of the United States has no authority or power to send his military into one of the adhering States for the purpose of preventing domestic violence at the polls unless he had been invited to do so by the State authorities, for the Constitution plainly and distinctly provides that he shall do it on application of the Legislature, if in session, and if that cannot be, then on the application of the Executive; and that is one of the wisest provisions in that sacred instrument. It is a provision intended to prevent a despotic President from interfering by armed force with the rights of the States and the liberties of the people. Mr. Justice Story, in his Commentaries on the Constitution, second volume, section eighteen hundred and twenty-five, page 633, speaking of this clause of the Constitution, says:

"It may not be amiss further to observe (in the language of another commentator) that every pretext for intermeddling with the domestic concerns of any State under color of protecting it against domestic violence is taken away by that part of the provision which renders an application from the Legislature or executive authority of the State endangered necessary to be made to the General Government before its interference can be at all proper. On the other hand, this article becomes an immense acquisition of strength and additional force to the aid of any State government in case of an internal rebellion or insurrection against lawful authority."

This learned commentator takes the very view of this clause of the Constitution that I have heretofore indicated. But for this provision of the Constitution a corrupt, venal, or ambitious President could by means of the military force, under some imaginary plea of domestic violence, invade any State in the Union on the eve of an election, and dictate the persons who should be returned as members of the other House of Congress, who should be returned as members of the Legislature, who should be returned as Governors of the States. In a word, if you allow him to use the army in this way without the invitation of the State authorities, a wicked and corrupt man would have it in his power to prostrate every State government in the Union, and to elect officers who would do his bidding, and thus overthrow the liberties of the people, and establish a consolidated despotism of which he would be the master.

Mr. President, after the few preliminary remarks which I have made, I will now proceed to the examination of the report made by the Committee on Military Affairs upon this bill.

REPORT OF COMMITTEE ON MILITARY AFFAIRS.

Mr. President, this bill, which was referred to the Committee on Military Affairs, came back to the Senate accompanied by a very voluminous adverse report. I have read the report with a great deal of care, and if I had not known that it was made by a committee composed of honorable Senators of this body, I never should have dreamed that such a document could emanate from a committee of the Senate of the United States. So far from meeting the case and discussing the bill fully, fairly, candidly, and impartially, the committee made a report of some fifty-two closely printed pages, almost every line of which is a labored defense of the President and the military authorities who had command in Kentucky, Maryland, and Delaware; and in order to make the defense of the military commanders and of the President complete, the report indulges in the harshest assaults upon every person whose name appears in the documents before the committee that at all complains or censures the military for their

unlawful and outrageous interference in the elections in those States.

The committee even travel out of the record to find objects for assault. The honorable Senator from Maryland [Mr. JOHNSON] took occasion some weeks since, in a debate that sprung up in this body, to make some remarks upon the election that had occurred in his State last fall. The committee in the report notice that, and I will read what they say of it:

"The recent Maryland election is a fruitful topic of complaint. The Governor and one of her Senators unite in denouncing it. The former, in his message, informs the Legislature that 'a part of the army which a generous people supplied for a very different purpose was on that day employed in stifling the freedom of election in a faithful State, intimidating its sworn officers, violating the constitutional rights of its loyal citizens, and obstructing the usual channels of communication between them and their Executive. And a Senator from Maryland has indulged in expressions which nothing but the most flagrant invasions of the elective franchise can excuse.

"But the weight of these imputations is seriously diminished by two considerations: both gentlemen owe their positions to an election conducted under the same auspices; both gentlemen are now on the losing side of the election which they impeach; and the country has not forgotten that it is the bad habit of the defeated partisans of the slavery interests to blacken the opponents whom they fail to defeat."

Mr. President, why step out of the way to make this assault upon the honorable Senator from Maryland? Nothing that the honorable Senator said was before the committee. They had before them the message and accompanying documents of the Governor of the State of Maryland, and upon that they could legitimately comment. They not only step out of the way to assault the Senator, but they impute to him most unworthy motives. Complaint is now made of the Maryland election, the committee say, because the Senator and the Governor are on the losing side. I, however, will not enter into any defense of the patriotic, able, and distinguished Senator from Maryland. He is in the Senate Chamber, and he is fully able to make his defense against all assaults and all assailants, whether they come from the Military Committee or from others in this Hall, or elsewhere. I will leave that matter to the honorable Senator himself. But I will simply say that I regard the assault as unjust, unwarrantable, and unworthy of a committee of this body. This is the first time I have ever seen in a report of a committee of this body an instance where they stepped out of the way to assail a Senator, and to attribute unworthy motives to him in order to strengthen and to build up the waning reputations of military commanders, whose conduct has been such that they must, in all after time, receive the condemnation of all honest, of all law-abiding and liberty-loving men.

Mr. President, allow me to read one or two extracts from this report. The committee, in the outset of the report, on the first page announce a proposition that is correct, and which I heartily approve. I will read it:

"The bill is founded upon the supposition that the military have in some instances interfered in an illegal or improper way with popular elections in the States, and seeks to prevent that evil for the future by the infliction of severe pains and penalties.

"That elections should be free from all violence and intimidation is an axiom of free government accepted by all, and so evident that it need not be discussed. Violence and threats of violence, and all disturbance, actual or threatened, calculated to keep the legal voter from the polls, or to constrain his free will and choice in exercising his right, are plainly incompatible with the principles on which our governments, whether State or Federal, rest."

I suppose the extract from the report which I have just read will receive the approval of every man who lives under a republican government or appreciates civil liberty.

I will undertake to show, and that too from the evidence that was before the committee, that the very infractions of right which they notice in the extract from the report had occurred, that the evidence was ample, full, and complete before them when they made the report recommending that the bill should not pass. Yes, sir, the Committee on Military Affairs had evidence, abundant evidence, in their possession, documents that they review in this very report, proving that the military had interfered in the most striking and unmistakable manner in the elections in the States of Kentucky and Maryland.

If the committee will adhere to the principle laid down in the extract which I have just read from their report, and will say that it is the duty of Congress by legislation to prevent the evil, then on the evidence I propose to present I shall have a right to demand their votes for this bill, or some bill to carry out the same views and objects.

The committee notice the statute of George II, passed in 1735, and they append a copy of it to the report.

I referred to that statute in the debate when this bill was up for reference; and the committee, in speaking of it, say :

"It cannot escape notice that the leading object of this ancient statute, as sufficiently evidenced by the preamble, was 'the preservation of the rights and liberties of the kingdom,' not their destruction. And the history of the time shows that the prohibition to keep military forces near places where there was an election of members of Parliament, arose from outrages practiced upon the electors by the ministers in posting troops so as to overawe them, and coerce them into the returning of candidates friendly to the ministerial party, and the supporters of prerogative against popular rights. And we are told that, so far did this party push their schemes, that in 1734, the year before the act was passed, the ministers, before the election took place, made out a list of the sixteen Scottish peers who were to be elected, which was approved by the Crown ; and that, among other foul means resorted to for securing their election, a battalion of the king's troops were drawn up in the court of Edinburg, contrary to custom, and without any apparent cause but that of overawing the electors. This outrage appears to have been the immediate occasion of the passage of the act. It was passed in the interest of liberty, and in resistance of the tyrannical schemes of the Crown and its flatterers to check its growth by stifling the voice of free election."

That is the comment the committee make upon that wise statute, and a most excellent commentary it is, and it is the very object recited in that statute which is to be effected by the passage of the bill under consideration. We desire to prevent the President and his officers from interfering in elections. We desire to preserve the ancient liberties of the people, and we know that that cannot be done unless elections are absolutely free. We desire that

the President shall not augment his power and overthrow the rights and liberties of the people by returning to the Congress of the United States or to the Legislature of the States men elected at the point of the bayonet, who are willing tools, ready to do his bidding. It is for that very purpose that we propose this bill. Conduct far more outrageous against the right of suffrage has occurred in these United States within the last two years than is represented by the committee in their comment upon this statute of George II, to have occurred in Great Britain.

INTERFERENCE IN KENTUCKY ELECTIONS.

The committee had before them an address and certain documents concerning elections in the State of Kentucky, upon which they comment at some length. So far as the military interference in the State of Kentucky is concerned, I will state the facts very briefly, and I will notice the report of the committee on that subject. The first palpable act of the interference of the military in regard to elections in that State occurred in the winter of 1863. During that winter there was a meeting of the Democratic party assembled at the capital of Kentucky for the purpose of nominating candidates for Governor and the other State offices. That convention was dispersed by a Colonel Gilbert, commanding a regiment of United States troops. I offered in this Chamber a resolution asking for a committee to investigate the conduct of that military officer in that interference with the right of the people to meet peaceably and to nominate candidates for office. The majority of the Senate declined to give me the committee. Afterwards, candidates nominated by one of the political organizations in Kentucky took the field. There were other persons, composed somewhat of both these parties, who determined, notwithstanding the interference at Frankfort, to organize the Democratic party. They did so by addressing a letter, which was signed by a large number of respectable gentlemen in the State, to Hon. Charles A. Wickliffe, requesting him to become a candidate for Governor. He did become a candidate for Governor, and other gentlemen became candidates for other State offices, and the State ticket was filled and regularly put on the track for the election to be held on the first Monday of August last.

Then it was that the military interfered in many parts of the State. In some parts of the State, I am happy to say, there was no interference or very little, except intimidation in consequence of military orders that had been issued. There was no direct and immediate interference by force, except in certain localities in the State. A committee of gentlemen who represented the organization that supported the Wickliffe ticket wrote an address to the people and to Congress in which they recited some of the acts of interference by the military authorities, which was presented to the Senate and referred to the Military Committee that had this bill in charge.

The committee in their report make very harsh and unjust remarks on the gentlemen who signed this address, and they do what is common with gentlemen on the other side of the Chamber. Whenever they want to break the force of an argument, or refute a fact, whenever they desire to defeat an object that they think is calculated to injure the party in power, they accuse those who make the charge of disloyalty, and they vainly think that is an answer to every argument and a refutation of every charge. The gentlemen who compose the committee that framed this address are charged as disloyal in the report of the committee, and the Military Committee embody in their report the letter of the gentlemen who invited Mr. Wickliffe to become a candidate. They harshly criticise that letter, and they pretend to regard the letter as disloyal. In order that these gentlemen may have a full vindication, as far as it is possible for me to make it, I will append their letter entire to my speech, and send it to the people; the letter will fully vindicate them from the unjust charges of the committee. I am ready and willing to maintain against all opposition the sentiments and principles set forth in that letter. To be sure, the writers of the letter very justly censure the Administration for unconstitutional acts. Among other things, it says;

"We hold this rebellion utterly unjustifiable in its inception, and the dissolution of the Union the greatest of calamities.

"We would use all just and constitutional means adapted to the suppression of the one and the restoration of the other."

That is the kind of language used by these gentlemen; and yet because they have had the patriotism, manhood, and courage to set forth the facts, and to prove beyond doubt the most unjustifiable and outrageous interference of the military in the elections in Kentucky, the Committee on Military Affairs, to get clear of and weaken the force of the facts and arguments set forth in the address, being wholly unable to meet them in fair and manly argument, or refute the facts, denounce the authors of the address as disloyal. Sir, I make bold to say, that so far as I know the gentlemen who signed that letter, and I know the most of them, there is not one of them who is or ever was disloyal. They are, each and every one of them, Union men. Their Unionism has been tested; they have been tried and not found wanting in fidelity to the constitutional Union of our fathers.

The committee are very much mistaken in some matters stated as fact in their report. On the 10th page they say:

"The writers, though pretending to hold the rebellion 'utterly unjustifiable in its inception,' leave a strong implication that it had become not unjustifiable, and seem to regard the employment of negro troops to 'make war upon the whites' in the rebel States as changing its original character from unjustifiable to the contrary. And such they, and their candidate undoubtedly regarded it, and had in contemplation to take measures of violence to resist it. At this time the recruiting of black troops, under the act of 1862, was in active progress in Kentucky, Tennessee, and other slaveholding districts."

Now, sir, at that time the enlisting of black troops was not actively going on in Kentucky. Every citizen of Kentucky knows that the committee are mistaken when they make that assertion. It has only been very recently that there has been any recruiting of negroes in Kentucky, and that, I believe, has been confined to the southern border of the State. And yet, sir, in order to make out a case against these gentlemen and against the Democratic candidate for Governor, Mr. Wickliffe, the committee assert as a fact what is not true. The committee, I have no doubt, were mistaken. I will not charge that they would intentionally misrepresent.

The committee base that assault upon the Democratic ticket and the gentlemen who signed that letter upon this clause in the letter:

"It is now obvious that the fixed purpose of the Administration is to arm the negroes of the South to make war upon the whites, and we hold it to be the duty of the people of Kentucky to enter against such a policy a solemn and most emphatic protest."

The committee construe that to mean the taking of violent measures against the Government! Every Union Legislature that has convened in Kentucky since this rebellion broke out has passed resolves protesting against the enlistment of that description of the population in the army. The people of Kentucky have uniformly protested against it; and yet, because the gentlemen who signed that letter also protest against it, the committee think that is highly revolutionary. Let me ask the Committee on Military Affairs if the people of any State in this Union have not the right to make their protest against any policy of the General Government? Most undoubtedly they have. If not they are the veriest slaves. Why, sir, it is done on some measure or another in almost every State in the Union every month during the session of Congress. It is the mode in which a free people make known their will, and arrest the attention of those who administer their Government affairs for the time being; and yet the Committee on Military Affairs think there is something criminal even in that!

The committee say that Mr. Wickliffe and the gentlemen who invited him to become a candidate desired rebels to vote. I will read that part of the report:

"The authors of the address, with commendable truthfulness, say: 'It is very frankly admitted that we hoped and expected to obtain the support of the great mass of the Southern rights men of the State. They were, for the most part, Democrats of long standing. Though classed by the adherents of the Administration as "disloyal," the great majority of them were not accessionists, and were entirely free from all complicity in the rebellion. So far from esteeming it a fault of which we should be ashamed, we regarded the effort to conciliate them, if it could be done without a sacrifice of principle on either side, as highly meritorious; and we now gratefully acknowledge the cordial support which that portion of our fellow-citizens were ready and anxious to yield to our platform and candidate whenever permitted to do so.'"

Upon that the committee remark:

"This is an express avowal of the purpose of the writers and of Mr. Wickliffe, their candidate, to obtain the votes, not only of loyal Democrats, but of persons who were open rebels, however numerous they might be. No one can deny this, and no one can deny that such a purpose was directly in the teeth not only of General Burnside's proclamation establishing martial law, but of the statute of Kentucky of March 11. It invited open enemies, whose hands were red with the blood of the defenders of the Government, and who were loaded with the spoils of plundered loyalists, to come to the polls and participate in the election of the officers of a loyal State! There is but one step, and that a short one, between this invitation and openly embracing the rebel cause."

The committee say that they invited those whose hands were red with the blood of Union-ists, and who were loaded with the spoils of the plundered friends of the Union, to come to the polls. Why, sir, never were a committee more mistaken. Those gentlemen did no such thing. They desired no rebel to vote. They asked the vote of no rebel. They desired that the constitution and election laws of Kentucky should be carried out, and faithfully administered by the officers appointed by the State for that purpose. I have read the extract from the address that called forth that comment. It says that they expected the support of the southern rights men of the State. The honorable Committee on Military Affairs must be most profoundly ignorant of the principles and feelings of those who at one time were called southern rights men—in Kentucky. That address tells you that the great majority of those southern rights men were not secessionists, and were entirely free from all complicity in the rebellion; and yet the Committee on Military Affairs say that the authors of this address invited those whose hands were red with the blood of Union men, and who were loaded with spoils taken from plundered loyalists, to come to the polls. The committee were drawing upon their fancy for their facts in making such a statement, and a most distempered fancy it must have been. They could not have been deluded by the words "southern rights," because this address states distinctly that the southern rights men were not secessionists, and were not implicated in the rebellion.

Allow me to say to the Senate at this point that the southern rights men in Kentucky never really amounted to a political organization. At the beginning of this rebellion, in the election of delegates to a border State convention, one portion of the candidates were called "Southern **rn** Rights" and the other "Union." The "Southern Rights" ticket, however, was withdrawn, and the "Union" ticket was elected without opposition. There might have been in some localities immediately after that some little party designation of that kind; but let me tell the Senate the southern rights men of Kentucky were, with a few exceptions, Peace Democrats. Many men who belonged to other political organizations heretofore now agree with them in sentiment. They were for the Constitution and the Union, were opposed to secession, were opposed to a dissolution of the Union, and they thought the only way in which that could be prevented was by peaceable means, by negotiation, compromise, and concession between the North and the South. They thought that war would result in a dissolution of the Union. It was because of their fervid devotion to the constitutional Union that they opposed the war.

They believed that war could cause the loss of hundreds of thousands of valuable lives; that the country would be laid waste, towns and cities destroyed; that untold millions of property would be destroyed; that it would result in the demoralization of our people; in a national debt of thousands of millions; in heavy and ruinous taxes upon the labor of the people that would consume and exhaust their substance; in an overthrow of the Constitution; in the destruction of the rights of the States; in a dissolution of the Union; in the loss of the liberty of the people; and in the prostration and ruin of both the North and the South.

The organization that put Mr. Wickliffe forward as the candidate was the Democratic party under its old name and under its old flag.

In this report the committee impugn the loyalty of Mr. Wickliffe; and upon what ground? Mr. Wickliffe was one of the first and stanchest Union men in the State of Kentucky. In the other end of this Capitol he voted men and money to carry on the war; and he never failed to do so until the last session, when he voted against an appropriation bill because the House would not insert a clause in it that the money should not be used for the purpose of freeing negroes and reducing States to provinces. It is well known that Mr. Wickliffe was a strong and warm friend of the war up to that time, until he thought the radical policy of the President was such as would destroy every hope of the restoration of the Union. He has never indicated an opposition to the war. He did vote against one appropriation bill, and assigned the reason I have stated; which, in my judgment, was a good and valid reason. Up to that time, however, I believe he voted all the men and all the money the Administration desired. When I say "all," I mean he generally voted in that way.

Well, sir, that sterling old patriot became the candidate of a party that were prevented from exercising the right of suffrage in Kentucky; and in order to justify that outrage and the striking of his name from the polls by the ruthless hand of the military, this committee say he is disloyal. I have no doubt if an angel of the Lord had appeared to the Committee on Military Affairs and told them there had been military interference in the elections in Maryland and Kentucky, that it was seen and known by all who were present at the polls, the writer of the report of the committee would have asserted that the angel was disloyal. Every man —I do not care how elevated his position or upright his standing in society, or how devoted he may have been in the past or the present to the Union—who asserts that there was interference in the elections, the committee say is disloyal, or they impute some unworthy motive to him.

In the letter addressed to Governor Wickliffe, requesting him to become a candidate, occurs this sentence:

"The Government has no more right to disregard the constitutions and laws of the States than the States have to disregard the Constitution and laws of the United States."

This proposition I did not suppose any constitutional lawyer would doubt. That both the States and the Federal Government are sovereign in their sphere, has been uniformly held by constitutional lawyers and the courts. It certainly follows that the General Government has no right to encroach upon the reserved rights of the States, and the States have no right to exercise the powers delegated to the General Government. The erudite writer of the report from the Committee on Military Affairs says this is "the precise doctrine of the nullifiers of 1832, and the very essence of secession." It is neither nullification nor secession, but a sound and constitutional principle. The committee ask, who are to judge between them? I answer, the courts.

The committee, in their report, most shamefully misrepresent the statements made in the address concerning the elections in Kentucky. The writer of the report claims to have carefully read the address. In speaking of the address the committee say:

"It narrates with an air of sorrow the fact that in August, 1862, Governor Magoffin, of Kentucky, resigned his executive trust for the purpose of relieving the people, and especially that portion of them known as southern rights men, who had been the peculiar objects of persecution."

It is not true that the address narrates the fact of the resignation with an air of sorrow. The address states the reasons which rendered the resignation of Governor Magoffin and the appointment of Governor Robinson desirable, and adds:

"These events gave rise to the most pleasing anticipations, which were strengthened by the first acts of the new regime."

Now, sir, in the report, W. A. Dudley, J. H. Harney, the editor of the Louisville Democrat, Judge W. F. Bullock, Judge J. F. Bullitt, Nat. Wolfe, R. R. White, and Dr. R. C. Palmer, strong Union men, who signed the address to the people and the Congress of the United States, are denounced as disloyal merely because they do not concur with the Committee on Military Affairs on this subject of the interference of the military in the elections in Kentucky. They knew that the military did interfere; they had the proof of that interference: many of them saw it; and as honest and brave men they dared to say it. They dared to arraign in proper language the usurpation of the military for their atrocious conduct in overthrowing the right of free speech and free suffrage; and to break the force of their declarations, the committee have nothing in reply but to impeach their loyalty. Why, sir, two or three of the gentlemen who signed that address were members of the Legislature for the last two years, and one of them at least cast his vote for the expatriation law of Kentucky to prevent rebels from voting. The signers of the address, upon which the committee make such an unfair, unjust, and unwarrantable assault, are the peers in every respect, socially, morally, and intellectually, of the Military

Committee of the Senate; as assault coming from that committee can injure them or tarnish their reputation for patriotism, truth, honor, or veracity in any community where the parties are known.

The gentlemen whose names are signed to the address are all denounced, or at least it is intimated that they are disloyal and unworthy of confidence and trust. Sir, among those names are the names of the most unflinching Union men in America. They are for the old Union as it was with the Constitution as it is. They are not like some of the members of the committee who make this report, for the Union only upon the condition that slavery shall not exist in it.

Mr. President, let us look a little further. The committee in this report say that the evils complained of in the address of the gentlemen whom I have named in Kentucky are merely imaginary. I will read that part of the report:

"So far as the committee have been able to ascertain, the evil which the bill is intended to remedy is almost wholly imaginary; and the fact that there is so little real ground for complaint against the military, considering the scenes of excitement and disorder in which they have been compelled to interpose, speaks loudly in praise of their justice and forbearance, and is high evidence of the impropriety of passing the bill."

Sir, let me say that honorable committee were never more mistaken in their lives than when they promulged the sentence just quoted. In the documents that were before the committee, the proof is abundant that the military did interfere and that gross violations of law took place in the Kentucky and Maryland elections, as I shall presently show.

I will call the attention of the Senate for a few moments to the military orders in Kentucky. The orders that prevented a free election in Kentucky were issued by various post commanders and commanders of districts in different parts of the State. General Boyle, commanding in western Kentucky, on the 25th of July, 1863, issued an order concerning seizing and impressing private property for military purposes, in which he instructed his officers that when it became necessary to take private property for the use of the army, those who were regarded as rebel sympathizers and who were opposed to a vigorous prosecution of the war, and furnishing men and money for that purpose, should be first taken, and vouchers should be given to them marked "loyal" or "disloyal." General Hartsuff issued a similar order in eastern Kentucky. It was said throughout the State by the party opposed to the Wickliffe ticket that their votes at the polls would be regarded as evidence as to whether they sympathized with the rebels or not. The fact of such orders being issued, and the general impression being spread in the community that those who voted the Wickliffe ticket would be regarded rebel sympathizers and their property taken for military purposes, prevented hundreds of men from voting.

Mr. HOWARD. Does the Senator refer to military orders?

Mr. POWELL. Yes, sir; to the military orders of General Boyle and General Hartsuff, the one commanding in eastern and the other in western Kentucky, which are made a part of this address.

▶ Mr. HOWARD. Will the Senator produce such an order?

Mr. POWELL. Yes, sir; I intend to produce it, and I intend to make it and all the military orders to which I refer a part of my speech. I shall produce every order to which I refer. Fortunately I have all that I desire to refer to in my possession. I will state furthermore that the committee had these orders to which I shall allude, in their possession when they made their report.

It was stated generally throughout the State, as every man' in Kentucky at all acquainted with affairs there at that time knows, that these orders——

Mr. HOWARD. I hope the Senator will allow me one word, as it is necessary to a clear understanding of the facts that he states. I understand the Senator to say that some military man in Kentucky issued an order to this effect, that the way in which the elector voted would be the proper mode of determining whether he was a loyal or a disloyal man. It was that order which I asked him to produce, if he has such a one.

Mr. POWELL. The Senator is mistaken.

Mr. HOWARD. Perhaps I misunderstood the Senator.

Mr. POWELL. I did not say such an order had been issued.

Mr. HOWARD. I understood the Senator to say such an order was issued.

Mr. POWELL. My statement is that such orders were issued as I have referred to.

Mr. HOWARD. The Senator will excuse me. I deny that there was any such order issued; and I put the Senator from Kentucky upon that issue to produce the evidence of the fact which he asserts.

Mr. POWELL. The Senator is denying something I did not assert. I have stated to the Senator that I did not say the order went to the extent that he understood. My statement was that orders were issued in the eastern and western departments of Kentucky saying that when necessary to take private property for the army, it should be taken from those who were denominated "sympathizers with the rebellion," and that those were classed as rebel sympathizers who were opposed to the war, and to furnishing men and money to carry it on. I said, in addition to that, that it was said throughout the State that the poll-books would indicate who were rebel sympathizers; that all who voted for Wickliffe would be classed as rebel sympathizers. That is what I said.

General Burnside, on the 31st of July, issued an order placing Kentucky under martial law and among other things declaring:

"As it is not the intention of the commanding general to interfere with the proper expression of public opinion, all discretion in the conduct of the election will be, as usual, in the hands of the legally appointed judges at the polls,

who will be held strictly responsible that no disloyal person be allowed to vote, and to this end the military power is ordered to give them its utmost support.

"The civil authority, civil courts, and business will not be suspended by this order. It is for the purpose only of protecting, if necessary, the rights of loyal citizens and the freedom of election."

General Burnside issued that order, as he states in a preamble to it, to prevent the rebel troops interfering in the election. There was no necessity for that order. At the time it was issued there were not in Kentucky more than about a thousand rebel soldiers, and they were calvary in one portion of the State in rapid retreat; and on the day of election there were no confederate soldiers in the State. General Burnside, at that time had under his command, it is said, fifty thousand men in Kentucky : so that when he issued that order there was no necessity whatever for it. The phraseology of the order itself, except that clause of it which says that he will hold the judges responsible, is in about as mild language as it could be under the circumstances.

But the committee go on to say that General Burnside had the authority and the power, and it was necessary to make that order placing Kentucky under martial law. That I deny. I will not now discuss the question as to whether General Burnside had the power to declare martial law. It is well known to the Senate that I hold there is no power in the Government, in the President, or any of his commanders, to declare martial law ; but if it did exist it should be confined to besieged cities and localities occupied by the army. But certainly there is no power to declare martial law in the adhering States, when they are not occupied by the force of the enemy.

It will be observed that the orders of General Boyle, General Hartsuff, General Shackleford, Colonel Foster, Lieutenant Colonel Johnson, General Asboth, and others, were issued before General Burnside's order placing the State under martial law ; so the excuse made by the committee in their report that the State was under martial law cannot avail those officers.

General Burnside plainly and palpably violated the Constitution of his country when he issued that order interfering with elections. He says the purpose was to prevent the rebels interfering in elections in that State. Let me ask, did the Governor of Kentucky invite General Burnside to bring his forces there to protect the election ? No, sir. The Legislature did not do it ; the Governor, in the language of the day a loyal man, never invited him to do it. Governor Robinson had no apprehension about the freedom of election there from rebel sources. I will read the preamble to this order of General Burnside:

"Whereas the State of Kentucky is invaded by a rebel force with the avowed intention of overawing the judges of elections, of intimidating the loyal voters, keeping them from the polls, and forcing the election of disloyal candidates at the election on the 3d of August ; and whereas the military power of the Government is the only force that can defeat this attempt, the State of Kentucky is hereby declared under martial law, and all military officers are commanded to aid the constituted authorities of the State in support of the laws and of the purity of suffrage as defined in the late proclamation of his Ex‐llenc‐ (h————‐ R‐l——‐‐‐ ‐‐

I intend to show, and that too from the proof that was before the Committee on Military Affairs, that the proclamation of General Burnside was not carried out as he made it; and his subordinates violated his proclamation and the proclamation of Governor Robinson which he made a part of it; and General Burnside, notwithstanding the fact was published throughout the whole State that his subordinates had violated his proclamation and the proclamation of the Governor, never censured or punished one of them for it, so far as I am advised.

Governor Robinson issued a proclamation on the 10th of July concerning the elections and he attached to it a statute law of the State of Kentucky entitled "An act to amend chapter fifteen of the Revised Statutes, entitled 'Citizens, expatriation, and aliens.'" That act of the Legislature declared all persons who had been or were engaged in the rebel armies or who had held office under the provisional government of Kentucky, or had given the rebels aid, expatriated, and that they were not entitled to any privileges of a citizen of the State after the act took effect. It took effect on the 11th of April, 1862. It was passed on the 11th of March, 1862, to take effect thirty days after its passage. That is the law of Kentucky. There could be no excuse then that there was no law of Kentucky to prevent rebels from voting.

But, sir, was the proclamation of the Governor of the State, inviting the attention of the judges of the election to that law, and directing them to enforce all the laws of the State, enforced by the military authority? I answer that it was not. The Committee on Military Affairs say that it was. There is a plain issue of facts; and I invite the Senate to the consideration of the proof. I will read the statement in the very language of the Committee on Military Affairs, and then no injustice can be done them. The committee, on the 12th page of their report, say:

"It is enough to say that, notwithstanding the manifest party exaggerations and distortion of fact of this pamphlet it does not allege that any loyal man who offered to vote for a loyal candidate was excluded or in any way molested by the military authorities. The orders of the subordinate commander were, so far as they are embodied in the pamphlet, and so far as we have been able to ascertain, in strict accordance with General Burnside's order and the statute of the State, which we have cited; and the pamphlet admits that these orders ' were carried out with rare fidelity by those to whom their execution was intrusted.' "

The address signed by the gentlemen from Kentucky alluded to does not admit that the order of General Burnside was carried out with strict fidelity. The committee are mistaken in that. The quotation from the address refers, not to the order of General Burnside, but to the orders issued by his subordinates, as a reference to the address itself will clearly show. In the address they say:

"General Burnside enforced the proclamation for the purpose of preserving the purity of elections, and (while himself threatening the judges of election should they permit a disloyal vote to be cast) directs that the soldiers shall

interfere no further than ma‐ l‐ nec‐ss‐ry to enable the judg‐s to discharge their duties under the laws of Kentucky. His subordinates threatened the judges and voters with confiscation, arrest, and imprisonment, and actually publish their orders and carry out their threats without punishment from the general or remonstrance from the Governor."

That is the charge in the address. Further on they say:

"The military orders before referred to were carried out with rare fidelity by those to whom their execution was intrusted."

What military orders? The orders of those subordinates. It clearly refers to them, and it says that they were carried out with rare fidelity. Many of these orders were in conflict with the order of General Burnside. The order of General Burnside cites the proclamation of the Governor, and says that the election must be carried on in obedience to the law as promulgated by the Governor. The Governor desired the election carried on under and by virtue of the laws of Kentucky, and in no other way whatever. What are the qualifications attached to voters by the law of Kentucky? Under the constitution of Kentucky, all white male persons twenty-one years old, who have had the necessary residence in their districts, and who have not been convicted of certain crimes, are qualified to vote. The law of expatriation declares that persons who do, or have done, certain things enumerated in it, shall be expatriated, be no longer citizens, and shall not enjoy any of the rights or privileges of citizens; and whenever any such person attempts to exercise any of the privileges of a citizen he may be required to negative on oath the expatriation provided in the act, and upon his failure or refusal to do so shall not be permitted to exercise any such right. What, then, is a voter to do under the law of Kentucky when he presents himself and demands to vote, if he should be challenged? He must swear that he has not been guilty of the offenses prescribed in the statute of March 11, 1862; that is, that he had not been engaged in the service of the provisional government of Kentucky; that he had not been in the rebel army; that he had not given them aid or assistance since the 11th day of April, 1862, the day on which the expatriation law went into effect. While on the subject of the date of the passage of the expatriation act, I will remark that the committee are in error when they say that the proclamation of Governor Robinson "was plainly necessary in order to call the immediate and earnest attention of the judges of election as well as the people to its important provisions which had been in force but three months." The date of the passage of the act is correctly given in the address as March 11, 1862, and it went into effect thirty days after its passage. The act had, therefore, been in force over fifteen months before Governor Robinson issued his proclamation on the 10th of July, 1863, and not but three months as stated by the committee. It is correctly stated in the report of the committee that Governor Magoffin resigned in August, 1862, and that this law was passed over his veto.

14

I cite this as a specimen of the reckless misrepresentation of facts of the writer of this report, in his effort to strike down the character of honorable gentlemen, in order to sustain those in power for a most unlawful and unjustifiable assault upon free suffrage.

The proposition, then, is very clear as to who were legal voters under the law of Kentucky. General Burnside said that the law must be carried out, as proclaimed by the Governor. What did his subordinates do? What were the orders issued by his subordinates? Here is an extract from one of them, issued by Lieutenant Colonel Thomas Johnson, at Smithland, Kentucky, July 16, 1863:

"Judges and clerks so appointed are hereby directed not to place the name of any person on the poll-books to be voted for at said election who is not a Union man, or who may be opposed to furnishing men and money for a vigorous prosecution of the war."

There is appended to that order an oath which varies from the oath prescribed by the law of Kentucky. The constitution and laws of Kentucky do not require that a man shall be in favor of furnishing men and money for a vigorous prosecution of the war to qualify him to hold office. In that particular the order is in conflict with the law of Kentucky and of the proclamation of General Burnside and Governor Robinson.

Here is also the order issued by General Asboth and others, west of the Tennessee river, in which they carry it still further. General Asboth in his order declares that both candidates and voters shall swear that they are willing to furnish men and money for a vigorous prosecution of the war before they are allowed to vote or stand for office.

Mr. HOWARD. Will the Senator inform me what pamphlet he is reading from? Is it the report of the committee?

Mr. POWELL. I am reading from the address on the Kentucky elections, which the committee had before them; for I do not intend in this connection to use any other evidence than that which was before the committee. I have other testimony, but I am now dealing with the report of the committee upon the evidence they had before them.

I have here the order of General Shackleford, issued at Russellville, Kentucky, and the order of Colonel Foster, issued at Henderson. I have also the orders issued by Generals Asboth and Hurlbut, west of the Tennessee river. On the back of the order of General Asboth is a statement signed by James S. Martin, colonel commanding post of Paducah, that he had the order executed in the counties of McCracken, Graves, Callaway, and Marshall.

From the evidence I have presented, is it not clear that the committee were mistaken when they said it was asserted in this address that the order of General Burnside had been faithfully carried out? They say the very converse, and they give the evidence and establish it beyond the possibility of a doubt by the official orders of the parties who made them and executed them.

It is apparent from the facts set forth in this address, notwithstanding the committee say that no loyal man was prevented from voting for a loyal candidate, that such was not the case. I suppose they will try to avoid this palpable misrepresentation by saying in reply that Mr. Wickliffe and the other candidates on his ticket were not loyal. No such false and slanderous charge against Mr. Wickliffe and other Democratic candidates will relieve the committee from this reckless misrepresentation. The proof is abundant in this address that in many of the counties the name of the whole Democratic ticket was stricken from the poll-book by the military authorities. In many voting places and in entire counties of Kentucky no man was allowed to vote for that ticket. In the county in which I live the names on the Democratic ticket were stricken from or not allowed to go on the poll books in three or four of the voting precincts. That fact is stated in the address. It is asserted that in one precinct of that county sixteen votes were cast, all for the Wickliffe ticket. The military then came there, took the poll-books from the judges and clerk, returned them to headquarters, and stopped the election; and yet the committee says no loyal man was prevented from voting for a loyal candidate! They establish to their own satisfaction, I suppose, that Governor Wickliffe and the men on the Democratic ticket were not loyal. They sit in judgment upon the loyalty of those men, and, for the unworthy purpose of sustaining, justifying, and excusing the President and the military authorities in the most flagrant, unconstitutional, unjustifiable, and atrocious assault upon the freedom of elections, they indulge in false and slanderous imputations and charges against the candidates of the Democratic party.

Sir, there is abundant evidence of the facts that I have indicated. Since the beginning of time there never was a more atrocious assault on free elections than took place in many of the counties in Kentucky. In many places the candidates were arrested. In the first congressional district Judge Trimble, the candidate for Congress, as loyal a man and as true to the Constitution and Union of his fathers as lives in the Union, was arrested by military authority. He was brought to the city of Henderson, a town just without his district, and there he was kept in military confinement near a month, until after the election was over. They told him that if he would decline being a candidate for Congress they would release him. He would not so degrade his manhood as to decline the canvass at the bidding of military tyrants and usurpers, and he was kept in prison. They found that he would be elected by a large majority notwithstanding his imprisonment, and then they sent the military over his district and had his name stricken from the polls in almost every voting precinct in the district. The gentleman who beat him got some four thousand votes in a district that polls about twenty thousand.

That is the way that a Union man was treated

Yes, sir, Judge Trimble, who has borne the name of a Union man all the time—who in the earliest conflicts in Kentucky was a Union man—was arrested, imprisoned for near a month, and turned out on the day after the election. With these facts before them, a committee of this Senate say that no loyal man was prevented voting for a loyal candidate!

Mr. ANDERSON, who now occupies the seat in Congress from the first district in Kentucky, frankly acknowledges that he was elected by the bayonets.

There was also arrested in that first congressional district of Kentucky Mr. Martin, a member of our last Legislature, and a Union man. He was a candidate for re-election in the counties of Lyon and Livingston. He was arrested and brought to the same city of Henderson, without the congressional district in which he lived, and he too was confined by the military until after the election; and then he and Judge Trimble were both released without any investigation whatever. The military told them that they would release them at any time if they would decline being candidates. Mr. Martin was beaten because the military would not allow him to be voted for. I suppose the committee regard Mr. Martin as disloyal. Mr. Martin, by occupation, was a steamboat pilot. He piloted the first gunboat bearing the flag of the United States that went up the Cumberland river during this rebellion. That is the way he exhibited his Unionism. He was elected as a Union man to our Legislature. He never was anything else; but like Judge Trimble, he did not agree in the abolition notions of President Lincoln; and for that offense they were stricken down and arrested by military authority, and their names stricken by the military from the poll-books. And yet the committee say that no loyal man was prevented from voting for a loyal candidate!

Mr. Blount Hodge, a true Union man, was a candidate for the State Senate. He resides in Livingston county. The military issued orders preventing his name going on the poll-books. These facts were before the committee when their report was made.

Mr. President, I will not indulge in any further vindication of the honorable gentlemen of Kentucky who are assailed by the committee. At home they need no defense; but I will say here in a single sentence that every charge, every aspersion, every insinuation against the loyalty, and patriotism, and the Unionism of those citizens is untrue, and that the committee are utterly mistaken when they make such charges. Such was the terrorism that prevailed throughout the State in consequence of military orders that many persons were deterred from voting, fearing if they voted the Democratic ticket their property would be taken by the military authorities for the use of the army. The military not only struck the names of candidates from the poll-books, but in many localities swore the voters themselves. Yes, sir, officers of the army and those in command of the soldiers at the polls, administered oaths to the voters. That evidently was in violation of General Burnside's orders. If the committee had examined the address they would see further that it is charged that persons who voted that ticket were pursued, arrested, and imprisoned. Such was the terrorism and interference by the military that Mr. Wickliffe, the Democratic candidate for Governor, in some six or seven of the strongest Democratic counties in the State, did not get a single vote, and in many other strong Democratic counties he received very few votes.

So much, sir, for the evidence contained in the address which was before the Committee on Military Affairs when they made this report. I have shown beyond the possibility of doubt from the evidence before the committee that they are utterly, wholly, and entirely mistaken in many of the matters stated as facts in their report. From the facts as we have them here in this address, if the committee adhere to the principle laid down in the beginning of their report which I have read they will vote for this bill.

But, Mr. President, fortunately for me and fortunately for the country, I have here the proof taken in a contested election in the second congressional district of Kentucky now pending before a committee of the House of Representatives, in which Colonel John H. McHenry contests the seat of Hon. GEORGE H. YEAMAN on the very ground that the election was not fair, but was interfered with by the military authority. The evidence in that case I know was not before the Committee on Military Affairs; but I will say that the evidence as given by witnesses of the highest respectability shows that interferences as great and greater than is set forth in the address which was before the Committee took place. It is proven that men, whom the witnesses testify were Union men and had always been Union men, were not permitted to vote for Colonel McHenry, who was a candidate for Congress.

Does anybody doubt the loyalty of Colonel McHenry? Sir, he has tested his loyalty on well-stricken fields. At Fort Donelson and at Shiloh he led his regiment into the thickest of the fight and bore aloft the banner of the Union. He received the commendations of all his superior officers. There was no colonel on that field of Shiloh that displayed more gallantry, bravery, or skill in the management of his regiment than Colonel McHenry. And yet, sir, Union men were prevented by the military from casting their votes for him; and I have the evidence before me taken in the contested election to which I have alluded.

I repeat, sir, the proof is here, and if any Senator now or hereafter shall doubt the truth of what I have said about these elections, I will read the testimony to the Senate.

INTERFERENCE IN MARYLAND ELECTION.

Mr. President, let us look into this report so far as it concerns Maryland. Two thirds of the report of the committee is devoted to the election in Maryland. I wish briefly to review the report so far as the Maryland election is concerned.

The committee have labored in their report to make a vindication of the President of the United States. General Schenck, and others for their interference in the election in Maryland, and in order to do that they assault the Governor of that State. The Governor of Maryland in his late message to the Legislature recites the interference with the election in that State, and in an appendix to his message he produces a great deal of proof, all of which was before the committee. I will read a few extracts from the message of Governor Bradford. I am happy to say that several members of the committee told me they never saw the report, and did not know what was in it. I wish I could say that much for all of them.

Mr. DAVIS. Maybe you can.

Mr. POWELL. I do not know whether I can or not. I should like to say that much for all of them. It is a report of which the committee and all honorable men should be heartily ashamed. The Governor says:

"A few days before that election a military order was issued from the army headquarters at Baltimore which in effect placed the polls under the surveillance and at the command of the military authority.

"I was the less prepared for any such order, from the fact that, though in frequent personal communication with the military authorities of the department, I had received no intimation whatever of such a proceeding or of any supposed necessity for it. In that part of the State against which the movement was to be more particularly directed (the Eastern Shore) there would seem to have been less necessity, as there certainly was less semblance of authority, than elsewhere; for while martial law had been proclaimed upon the Western Shore of the State in June last, and had not been repealed up to the day of election, upon the Eastern Shore it had never been proclaimed at all."

In the case of Kentucky, the committee justify the interference in the elections on the ground that General Burnside had declared martial law in that State. Martial law seems to have been declared by General Burnside for the purpose of giving his subordinates and their justifiers an excuse for their unlawful and outrageous conduct. As I have before shown, the orders of his subordinates were issued before he placed the State under martial law. On the Eastern shore of Maryland, Governor Bradford tells you, there was no martial law declared. Therefore General Schenck, and those acting under his authority, for their doings on the Eastern Shore of Maryland cannot be shielded and protected by the panoply of martial law. The Governor goes on to say, after speaking of the President modifying the order:

"Prominent among the provost marshals to whom the execution of this order was in part committed were several who were themselves candidates for important offices.

"These marshals, appointed for the purpose of the militia enrollment and draft, were placed by the law creating them under the control of the Provost Marshal General, but, to insure the right to employ them about this election order, special authority was obtained from Washington to place them for the time being under the orders of the military authorities."

Here we find that these provost marshals, many of whom were candidates for office, were

among the actors in this scene of interfering with the elections in Maryland.

"I, therefore, on the Monday evening preceding the election, issued a proclamation giving them this assurance, a copy of which is herewith submitted."

Saying that they must carry out the election in accordance with the law.

"Before the following morning military orders were sent to the Eastern Shore directing its circulation to be suppressed, the public papers were forbidden to publish it, and an embargo laid on all the steamers in port trading with that part of the State, lest they might carry it."

Here we find General Schenck suppressing as far as he could the circulation of the proclamation of the Governor to the people of the State. We find him laying an embargo on boats and the regular business of the State, for fear they might carry this proclamation to the people for whom it was intended. What was the reason for this interference? Governor Bradford in his message and in his proclamation says there was no necessity whatever for it. I do not suppose the loyalty of Governor Bradford was ever doubted until in an evil hour he fell into the hands of the Committee of the Senate on Military Affairs; and then, in order to shield the guilty culprits who had overthrown the constitution and laws of Maryland in one of the most vital parts, they attempt to strike down and blast the reputation of a loyal Governor of an adhering State. To what base uses will not the adherents of power lend themselves! There stands the message saying that these interferences have taken place, and in order to shield the guilty culprits the reputation of Governor Bradford has to be destroyed. He is charged with usurpation; his loyalty is questioned, his patriotism doubted; and he is gently admonished that he ought to be an imate of a prison. The committee say, "the Governor bitterly complains of the suppression of his proclamation, instead of gratefully acknowledging the moderation which arrested its circulation instead of its author." Why these charges of usurpation? Why these threats of imprisonment? Is it to seal the lips of those who dare speak of the usurpations and crimes of the party in power? A faithful Governor of an adhering State makes an effort to see that the laws of his State are faithfully executed, and he is denounced as a usurper, and gently reminded of imprisonment.

Did Governor Bradford invite General Schenck, or the President of the United States, or any other military authority, to bring soldiers there for the purpose of preventing domestic violence in Maryland? No, sir; he says he did not. The clause of the Constitution that I have heretofore read and commented on declares that the United States authorities shall only interfere when the Legislature or the Executive of the State demand it, to prevent invasion or domestic violence. Were there any rebel troops in Maryland? The imbecile Burnside, the jailer of Vallandigham, had the excuse of about one thousand rebel soldiers, who were rapidly running out of Kentucky, while he had about fifty thousand men under his control to fight them.

He had that impotent and lame excuse for placing Kentucky under martial law. But, sir, I have not yet heard that there were any rebel soldiers in Maryland; and yet, in violation of the Constitution of the United States, we find that soldiers were sent to the polls to interfere in the elections in that State; and they did interfere, notwithstanding the Committee on Military Affairs cannot find it out, although they had all the testimony before them that is appended to the message of Governor Bradford. The Governor goes on to say:

" How far it accomplished the purpose claimed for it, or how far my anticipations of the consequences of the order and the abuses to which it would lead were realized, will appear by a brief reference to some of the transactions connected with its execution. These abuses commenced even before the opening of the polls. On the day preceding the election, the officer in command of the regiment which had been distributed among the counties of the Eastern Shore, and who had himself landed in Kent county, commenced his operations by arresting and sending across the bay some ten or more of the most estimable and distinguished of its citizens, including several of the most steadfast and uncompromising loyalists of the shore. The jail of the county was entered, the jailer seized, imprisoned, and afterwards sent to Baltimore, and prisoners confined therein under indictment were set at liberty. The commanding officer referred to gave the first clue to the character of the disloyalty against which he considered himself as particularly commissioned, by printing and publishing a proclamation in which, referring to the election to take place next day, he invited all the truly loyal to avail themselves of that opportunity and establish their loyalty ' by giving a full and ardent support to the whole Government ticket upon the platform adopted by the Union League convention,' declaring that ' none other is recognized by the Federal authorities as loyal or worthy of the support of any one who desires the peace and restoration of the Union.' "

There you see this lieutenant colonel issues his proclamation in which he invites the people to come up and establish their loyalty by giving a full and ardent support to the whole Government ticket, upon the platform adopted by the Union League convention, declaring that none other is recognized by the Federal authorities as loyal or worthy the support of any one ; and yet the Committee on Military Affairs assert that there was no interference! The Governor further says:

" Major General Dix, when in command of this Department, at the time of the election in 1861, and when, too, rebellion was backed by its organized supporters in our very midst, took the true and statesmanlike view of the policy proper for such an occasion when, in directing his provost marshal, he said that while there was no difficulty in controlling Maryland by force, that this was not what was wanted, but that he wished to control it by the power of opinion, and that to satisfy the country that the people were on our side, we must leave them to an unbiased expression of their wishes. They were left to that unbiased expression, and such was its character that I had supposed no one would still require evidence of their loyalty.
" General Dix was even appealed to by some of the judges of election to authorize an oath to voters of doubtful loyalty, and although it appears from the tenor of his reply that the oath suggested was nothing more than an oath to support the Constitution of the United States, he refused to order it, saying to them, among other things, ' The constitution and laws of Maryland provide for the exercise of the elective franchise by regulations with which I have no right to interfere.' "

General Dix spoke wisely. President Lincoln, however, the Commander-in-Chief of the Army, did not so regard it. He did interfere with this very matter, and without being requested by Governor Bradford to do so. So far from re-

questing the President, as the Constitution authorized him to do when he desired the force of the United States to protect the State against invasion or domestic violence, he complained of the military being sent there. The President did not have the sanction of Governor Bradford, but did it against his protest, for he asked the President to repeal the order, and he did modify the order of General Schenck in one or two particulars, but really made it very little better than it was, and his modifications were disregarded in many localities in the State.

Sir, we find the President himself meddling in this matter of elections. He, as well as his chosen instrument, General Schenck, and all the other instrumentalities in the military service throughout that State, was in the exercise of the harshest usurpations against the loyal people of that State. Governor Bradford, in his message and proclamation, tells you that there were no candidates on the Eastern Shore but Union men, so far as he was advised ; that throughout all Maryland there were not rebels or rebel sympathizers enough to affect the elections, except, perhaps, in one district, and that was not the district of which complaint was made. Why, sir, John W. Crisfield, known to many Senators here, an able and honored member of the last House of Representatives, was a candidate for re-election, known always as a Union man. He it was whom the soldiers of the Army of the United States, with the direct knowledge of the President of the United States, prevented receiving a re-election. I do not think there is a doubt about the re-election of Mr. Crisfield in the district on the Eastern Shore, had the military not interfered.

In this Maryland case you cannot throw off the responsibility upon Schenck, nor upon Colonel Tevis, or other subordinates. You have the President most directly implicated. Here he is upon the record, violating the Constitution of his country by interfering with elections in States in order to return menials and miserable creatures to Congress who would do his bidding ; and I arraign him for this offense before the Senate of the United States and the American people. I brush away the trash and come right to the Commander-in-Chief himself, and charge him, upon the most indubitable testimony, with trampling under foot the most inestimable right of free suffrage and free election, and, in order to effect his object, committing a palpable violation of the Constitution of the United States, which he was sworn to support.

There, sir, these documents place the President, and there is no power that can ever rescue him from that position. I regret that it is so. I regret that I have to state in my place as a Senator that the Executive, whom a grateful people have elevated to power and charged to take care that the laws are faithfully executed, has exhibited such infidelity to his oath and made such vital stabs on the Constitution of his country and on the free suffrage of the people ; but truth compels me to make the charge. Here are the proofs ample to sustain it. Here are the President's own letters and orders. Out of his own mouth we condemn him. He cannot plead as an excuse that the Governor of Maryland desired it, for the Governor protested against it and appealed to him to relieve the State from that disgrace. He refused to do it. He cannot get off on the ground that Governor Bradford is disloyal. Oh, no; not at all. The Governor's truth, patriotism, and loyalty are above suspicion in the minds of all patriotic and honest men, notwithstanding the assault of the writer of the report of the Committee on Military Affairs.

But the learned Committee on Military Affairs try to weaken the force of the statements of Governor Bradford and of the honorable Senator from Maryland, by saying that they were elected under similar circumstances. Suppose they were, sir; it only shows the greater necessity for the passage of the bill that I propose. If forty Governors were elected under similar circumstances, that fact would afford forty additional reasons why this bill should pass. If military force was used to elect Governor Bradford and to place the honorable Senator from Maryland in his seat here, that is no reason why others should be elected by such unlawful and outrageous influences. Two wrongs never made a right.

The report goes on to say:

"It is not true that ' the military, aided by the provost marshal's, were to arrest voters whom they might consider as loyal approaching or hanging about the polls.' "

That was certainly in General Schenck's original order. The President, however, modified that part of it. The modification, as I have before stated, was disregarded.

"It is not true that ' a prescribed form of oath was furnished, without taking which no one, if challenged, could vote.' "

Now I think anybody who will read the order of General Schenck, and read that oath, must think the committee mistaken in making the assertion. General Schenck, after his first order and the proclamation of Governor Bradford were issued, plainly indicated in an address to the loyal people of Maryland, dated November 3, 1863, that those who were challenged could not vote except by taking the oath. The indication is clear that they could not do it otherwise; and the military were sent, they say, to enforce that order, to compel the oath and to protect the judges! Is that what they did? I will show you presently that it is not. Speaking of the Governor's proclamation, the report says:

"That proclamation was much more liable to the charge of illegality than the order of which it complained."

The committee charge that the proclamation of Governor Bradford was illegal, more so than General Schenck's order. There can be no doubt about the illegality of General Schenck's order. The committee are even divested, so far as the Eastern Shore is concerned, of the excuse that there was martial law there. They are divested of another excuse that they might

have, that Governor Bradford asked the interposition of the Federal Army to protect the State against invasion or domestic violence, for he not only did not ask it, as the Constitution required, (the Legislature not being in session,) before it could be lawfully furnished, but he protested against it. The Governor had the right to issue his proclamation. The learned and erudite committee say:

"The law of Maryland charges the Governor with no authority over elections, and vests him with no right to instruct the judges of election in the law of their duty."

It was left to the Military Committee of this honorable Senate, a learned committee, to be sure, to make the discovery that the Governor of Maryland had no constitutional authority to issue a proclamation concerning elections! They say the laws do not charge him with it. Why, sir, I see in the Constitution of Maryland, which I have before me, that it is written in the tenth section of the second article that the Governor "shall take care that the laws be faithfully executed." And yet, because he advised the judges to execute the law—for that is all the Governor did—the honorable Committee on Military Affairs call him a usurper. They say he had no lawful right to do it.

Consistency is said to be something of a virtue, and the Senate will be astonished when I tell them that this committee commend Governor Robinson for issuing his proclamation in Kentucky, and setting forth the law of expatriation from Kentucky, and urging upon the judges of election the strict observance of all the laws of the State regulating elections, and they censure soundly the gentlemen in Kentucky who issued the address from which I have read, because they took some exception to Governor Robinson's proclamation. The committee think the proclamation of Governor Robinson at that time was highly commendable and proper, and then they say that Governor Bradford had no lawful authority to issue his proclamation! To what miserable quibbles and inconsistencies those who defend tyrants and usurpers are driven!

The gentlemen who signed the address that was before the committee censured the Governor of Kentucky because he had not cited and published all the laws of Kentucky concerning elections but only published one. But the Governor of Maryland in his proclamation does tell the judges to execute all the laws, and the committee think that is a usurpation. When the committee think they can make an assault on the gentlemen who wrote this address, they eulogize Governor Robinson and censure the gentlemen who signed the Kentucky address; but when they come to Maryland, in order to destroy a witness against Abraham Lincoln, Schenck and others, they charge Governor Bradford with doing things without any warrant of law. I suppose there is not a Senator here who does not know that every Governor is charged to see that the laws of the Commonwealth over which he presides are faithfully executed. The election laws are a part of the laws of the State. But that is not all. The committee say of Governor Bradford:

"This proclamation was, therefore, a palpable usurpation."

Sir, the Military Committee of the Senate pronounces a proclamation of the Governor calling the attention of the judges of election to the laws of that State and urging them to see the laws executed, and to see that the elections were absolutely free, a usurpation. Governor Bradford did it in obedience to the constitution of his State, and if he had not done it under the circumstances he would have been delinquent and fallen far short of the discharge of his duties as a wise, virtuous, and patriotic Governor. If that is a usurpation, allow me to ask the honorable Committee on Military Affairs what would they call the act of President Lincoln and General Schenck and his subordinates? They issued orders concerning elections in Maryland. They were not authorized by any constitution or any law to do it. They did it in palpable, direct violation of the Constitution of the United States, because the Governor of Maryland had not invited their interposition. They prescribed oaths to to be taken unknown to the constitution and the laws of Maryland, thus prescribing the qualifications of voters to the extent at least of excluding all who would not take an oath unknown to their laws. And then, sir, we find this sentence in this most learned report:

"The execution of the order was as fair and upright as the order itself was legal and its purpose honest."

I understand the committee to assert that the order was constitutional and legal, and that its execution was fair and upright. A more palpable usurpation never existed than the issuing of the order. I have shown, and shown it, too, from the Constitution of the United States, that it was a violation of that sacred instrument. They had no plea of martial law. From the message of the Governor of Maryland we learn there was no plea of necessity, that plea which tyrants always urge. But they say the execution of the order was fair and upright. Now, Mr. President, the Committee on Military Affairs had before them the message of the Governor of Maryland, with the documents appended. They comment on them, they quote them, they refer to them; so, then, they cannot say that the evidence was not before them. About one third of the report is devoted to combatting this message and the evidence accompanying it. Now let us see what the evidence is they had before them. I have given you the statement of the Governor. He says the provost marshals were many of them candidates, and that men were prevented from voting by the military. Now look at the evidence, and see how far the committee are correct in their statement that the order was carried out in a fair and upright manner. I will read to the Senate the order referred to by his Excellency Governor Bradford, made by one of the military officers on the Eastern Shore:

HEADQUARTERS THIRD MARYLAND CAVALRY,
CHESTERTOWN, November 3, 1863.

Whereas the President of the United States, in reply to a letter addressed to him by Hon. Thomas Swann, of Baltimore city, has stated that all loyal qualified voters should have a right to vote, it therefore becomes every truly loyal citizen to avail himself of the present opportunity offered to place himself honorably upon the record or poll-book at the approaching election, by giving a full and ardent support to the whole Government ticket, upon the platform adopted by the Union League convention. None other is recognized by the Federal authorities as loyal or worthy of the support of any one who desires the peace and restoration of this Union.

CHARLES CARROLL TEVIS,
Lieutenant Colonel Commanding.

What must be thought of an officer who issues an order declaring in substance that none would be regarded as true and loyal Union men unless they voted the ticket placed upon the platform of the Loyal League? I do not know precisely what these Loyal Leagues are, but I understand they are some kind of secret, oath-bound political society. That, then, is the platform that this officer tells you is the only one that the Government recognizes. That of itself would be enough to prevent a fair and upright election. There is abundant proof accompanying the Governor's message that loyal men were prevented from voting by the soldiers. The proof is that men offered to vote the Crisfield ticket, and that they were prevented and driven off by force by the soldiers, and that afterwards the yellow or Creswell ticket, the ticket of the loyal leaguers, was placed in their hands, and they were forced to vote it. I will read a sentence or two from the Governor's message and documents. It says:

"Mr. Davis came to vote, and Henderson said, 'You can't vote.' He asked Davis 'Will you take the oath?' He said 'Yes:' and as we were about to administer the oath prescribed in General Schenck's order No. 53, which had been a test for Crisfield voters, Mr. Henderson ordered Sergeant Tonitt to arrest Davis and take him in custody, and thus Davis left the poll without voting. Another man came up with a Crisfield ticket in his hand and offered to vote, and Henderson said to us, 'If you take that man's ticket I will take the ballot-box from you;' and thus he did not vote. A man named John Pruth came to vote, but was challenged by some one and refused to take the oath, was turned down, but after a time came with a Creswell ticket, and Henderson ordered us to take his ticket.

That is the statement of one of the election judges.

At this point the honorable Senator gave way to a motion to adjourn.

FRIDAY, *March* 4, 1864.

Mr. POWELL. Mr. President, when the Senate adjourned yesterday evening I was commenting upon this clause in the report of the committee:

"The execution of the order was as fair and upright as the order itself was legal and its purpose honest."

I was endeavoring to show by the testimony before the committee that they were mistaken in thinking the order was fairly executed. I will read from the report of the committee another enunciation on this subject, and then I shall proceed to show that they were entirely mistaken in their assertions. On the 28th page of the report I find the following, referring to the election in the first congressional district of Maryland :

There does not appear to your committee the least reason to believe that a single person was hindered from voting by the military in the first congressional district who had not been engaged in the rebel service or in aiding and abetting them, nor that the judges excluded any voter who proved his citizenship by confessing its obligations under oath."

The Committee on Military Affairs had before them the message of the Governor of Maryland and the documents appended to it concerning the election in that State; and from those documents, from the proofs before the committee, I will establish beyond doubt that the committee are in error in both the statements in the report that I have read. I have here a statement signed by ten gentlemen, who I am informed are gentlemen of the highest respectability, living on the Eastern Shore of Maryland, addressed to Governor Bradford, from which I will read an extract:

" Throughout the day special pains were taken to put obstacles in the way of those voting the conservative Union ticket, such as challenging them, making them take the oath, and this even in the case of old gray-headed Union men, while notorious sympathizers with the rebellion were permitted to vote unchallenged, provided they voted the emancipation ticket. One case which created some excitement at the time deserves particular notice. A man who has been always regarded as a sympathiser with the South went up to vote with an unconditional Union ticket in his hand, and was challenged by a Union man. The person desiring to vote then declared that he would not take the oath, and that if he had to take the oath he would not vote. And yet, with the military order in full force, whenever the independent Union ticket was presented, this man was permitted to vote! And more than this, the Union citizen who challenged the above party was threatened with arrest by a candidate on the emancipation ticket for merely carrying out the military order which this candidate and his friends were strenuously upholding. One of the judges of election declared that the fact of a voter having an unconditional Union ticket in his hand was an evidence of his loyalty; and in the case above cited, as your Excellency will notice, this decision was fully carried out. These are but a part, a small part, of the events of the day. In other districts not only were persons refused permission to take the oath and vote, but the part of the order which was modified by the President was fully carried out as it was promulgated. Voters were driven away and told if they returned they would be arrested. A part of the cavalry regiment, in some districts, were permitted to vote, although not residents of the county on the shore, because they were soldiers !"

That evidence was before the committee when they made the report. In the memorial of the defeated candidates in Kent county, on the 69th page of the message and accompanying documents, I find the following:

· "In one other of the districts the polls were not opened until nearly twelve o'clock, in direct violation of the laws of the State, when many of the voters of the district had returned to their homes. At the polls of four of the districts of the county a military officer was stationed near the judges of election, and challenged and rejected voters in many instances without referring to the judges, whose right and duty it was to decide upon the legality of such votes. The result of such unprecedented proceedings was that the voters of the county were impressed with the conviction that the election was entirely under the control of the military power of the United States, and that they would not be permitted to vote unless the caprice of the officers in command should sanction it, or they would vote for the candidates indicated by the order of Colonel Tevis.'"

On the 69th page of the message and accompanying documents I find the following state-

ment by Thomas Sudler, one of the judges of election in Somerset county:

" I was one of the first at the voting place; I found the judges of election and certain soldiers; the polls were not then open. I saw the judges reading a paper, which I ascertained was the 'Order No. 53' issued by General Schenck. I then displayed the proclamation of the Governor of Maryland, which had reached me by express the signing previous. The officers in charge of the soldiers asked me to read it, which I did. The sergeant—the officer mentioned above—then said : ' I have orders to enforce General Schenck's order No. 53." I inquired further of the sergeant concerning his order. The sergeant replied that before he left the camp at Princess Anne, and before the proclamation had been received by the captain of the whole body of troops in this camp, he received orders to enforce the Order No. 53"—

That was General Schenck's order—

"to challenge every voter, to examine all tickets offered, to administer the oath contained in Order No. 53, and to decline to allow any ticket but the yellow or Creswell ticket to be polled." * * * * " There were very few voters at the polls. The mass of the people were deterred from coming out by fear of the soldiers, who were reported to have received orders to arrest all who voted for Mr. Crisfield."

I will now read from the statement of Cyrus L. Jones, on the 72d page;

" In response to a question I asked him, the sergeant pulled out of his pocket a yellow or Creswell ticket, and said, ' This is the only ticket that shall be voted to-day.' I then mentioned that I had received the proclamation of Governor Bradford, which had that very morning reached me by express, and called his attention to it. The sergeant said he ' had nothing to do with the Governor's proclamation,' that his orders ' were above that ;' and added that the orders of his provost marshal had to be obeyed that day. I said, if the oath is to be administered to all who come, you will have to do it. Our orders are to allow every one twenty-one years old to vote. I called the attention of my brother judges, saying, ' There will be a hereafter to this.' The sergeant then guarded the window through which the ballots were handed in to be put in the ballot-box with soldiers, took his place at the window, and rejected all who would not vote the yellow or Creswell ticket. He did not permit a single ticket of any other description to be polled, although I saw two men make several attempts, at different times during the day, to vote a ticket with Mr. Crisfield's name on it, and many other men were intimidated from offering to vote."

I will now read an extract from the statement of Mr. J. H. Tarr, dated Salisbury, November 12, 1863:

" When I approached the window to deposit my ballot, it being on white paper, and also knowing I was favorable to the election of Hon. J. W. Crisfield for Congress, Lt. D. Collier, deputy provost marshal, challenged my vote. I inquired upon what ground. He answered that I was a copperhead, and no damned copperhead should vote that day. He referred to General Schenck's order. I produced your able and ever to be respected proclamation, and read it aloud to the judges, one of whom was a candidate for judge of the orphans' court. His reply was, 'Damn the proclamation.' I then requested him to define loyalty, stating at the same time I would affirm to the condition of the oath as prescribed. This was refused, and I was ordered away from the polls. I left without voting."

Mr. Tarr goes on further to state:

" From the first outbreak to the present moment I have been for the Union, and am still for the Union. I voted for you, and have never regretted it."

This is addressed to Governor Bradford:

" I stand where I have always stood, for ' Union, the Constitution, and the enforcement of the laws,' with no sympathy for the rebellion."

That man, although he affirmed he was willing to take the oath, and says that he is a Union man with no sympathy for the rebellion, was refused his vote under the orders of this deputy provost marshal.

Mr. HOWARD. I rise to inquire of the Senator from Kentucky what book he is reading from?

Mr. POWELL. I am reading from a pamphlet entitled "Message of Governor Bradford to the General Assembly of Maryland, with documents, &c." The extracts I am now reading are from the documents accompanying the message. Here is an extract from a letter by Charles Cole to Governor Bradford, inclosing a certificate from Lewis F. Wachter:

"Inclosed is a certificate from Lewis F. Wachter, a highly respectable farmer of Frederick election district, showing how he was treated on election day, and compelled to vote against his sentiments. I saw that man pushed from the voting place and kicked at as he was descending the steps leading into the court-house, where the polls were held, and after he had retired a short distance I saw the same soldier who kicked at him seize him by the arm, thrust an 'Unconditional ticket' into his hand, and, with the assistance of another soldier, compel him to return and vote the ticket which had been placed in his hand."

And yet, with all these facts before them, the honorable Committee on Military Affairs in their report say that the election was fair, and that no Union man who would take the oath was prevented from voting. This Mr. Wachter in his certificate says:

"I hereby certify that I offered to vote the conservative Union ticket at the north polls, in the city of Frederick, on Wednesday, the 4th day of November, 1863, and that a soldier objected to my voting on the ground of disloyalty; that my ticket was taken from my hand at the same time by a soldier, and that I left the polls and had not proceeded further than thirty or forty feet before a soldier, whose name I am informed is Marcellus Shaffuer, came up to me and said, 'Here, you will be entitled to a vote; now come and vote;' at the same time putting an Unconditional ticket into my hand, and seizing me by one of my arms, and another soldier by the other, I was forced again back to the polls through fear of personal violence, and compelled to vote against my sentiments."

Mr. President, how the committee could have put the statements I have heretofore read in their report with this evidence before them, is a matter most astonishing to me. The writer of the report reviews the message of Governor Bradford and the evidence accompanying it, reviews it elaborately, and after that review makes the statements. I have quoted from the report. The motive that actuated the writer of the report to make the statements alluded to I leave the Senate to determine.

Mr. President, it is clear from the statements I have read that there was a most unwarrantable and unjustifiable interference with the election in the State of Maryland. The judges were prevented from executing the laws. In many cases they were imprisoned. Loyal men were forced from the polls when they attempted to vote the Crisfield ticket, and afterwards forced back to the polls and compelled to vote the Creswell ticket. In some places the Crisfield ticket was not allowed to be voted. Disloyal men, or men whose loyalty at least was suspected, were allowed to vote the yellow or Creswell ticket. Even when they were challenged, the soldiers would not permit them to be sworn; and in one case they threatened to take the ballot-box if the vote was not taken. Upon what ground the committee can base the assertion in their report that this election was con-

ducted fairly, and that no person who was a loyal citizen and would take the oath was prevented from voting, I am wholly unable to comprehend.

Sir, we might well inquire why it was that at that particular juncture of Maryland affairs the military should be scattered all over that region of country? Were there any rebel soldiers there? Was the State of Maryland invaded? No, sir; they had no such excuse as General Burnside claimed for declaring martial law in Kentucky. Why was it done? The object is clear and manifest. Those soldiers were sent there for the purpose of carrying the elections in favor of the Administration. I read some time ago, and I regret that I have not got it before me now, an extract taken from the Boston Commonwealth, a leading Administration party paper, in which it complained somewhat of the conduct of the soldiery in the border State elections, and called them "irregularities," but said the Administration had been so negligent in allowing the Democrats to elect so many members of Congress in the previous elections that they were compelled to interfere in the border States in order to maintain a majority in the other end of this Capitol; and upon that ground they excused it. That was the reason the iron hand of the military was laid upon the people of the border States; to compel them to send members of Congress to this Capitol who were opposed to the sentiments of the people. It was done by the Administration for the purpose of having a majority in their favor in the other House.

But, sir, did anybody then, or does anybody now, pretend to say that the people of Maryland were not loyal? I will read to you what their Governor says on that subject. The writer of the report, in order to bolster up the President, General Schenck, and others in authority, assails and attempts to destroy the reputation of Governor Bradford and everybody who testifies in reference to these violations of the law in those States. The destruction of the reputations of those who know and have spoken of these disgraceful and wicked usurpations is the only means by which they can escape from that damning infamy which must in all time accompany them. What does Governor Bradford say in regard to the loyalty of the people of Maryland?

"It is a well-known fact, that with perhaps one single exception, there is not a congressional candidate in this State whose loyalty is questionable, and in not a county in the State outside of the same congressional district is there, I believe, a candidate for the Legislature or any State office whose loyalty is not equally undoubted."

He says further:

"For more than two years past there never has been a time when, if every traitor and every treasonable sympathizer in the State had voted, they could have controlled, whoever might have been their candidates, in a single department of the State, or jeoparded the success of the General Government. No State in the Union has been or is now actuated by more heartfelt and unwavering loyalty than Maryland—a loyalty intensified and purified by the ordeal through which it has passed."

That is what the Governor says in his proclamation. General Schenck, in a paper that he issued in reply to this proclamation of the Governor's, indorses the loyalty of the people of Maryland, in this language:

"Governor Bradford himself cannot appreciate more highly than I do, the sterling loyalty of the great majority of the people of Maryland."

General Schenck himself says that a great majority of the people of Maryland are loyal. Where, then, was the necessity for this military foray upon them upon the day of election? It can only be accounted for by the reason that I have stated: the Administration did it for the purpose of preventing a free election in Maryland, and in order to send to the other end of this Capitol and elect as officers of that State government, men who were willing to do the bidding of the Executive. It was for that, and for nothing else, that it was done. There never was a greater outrage on any people on earth than was committed on the loyal people of Maryland in their last election.

I read yesterday the law of the free commonwealth of Athens on this subject. The Athenians were so watchful and so jealous of the right of free suffrage that a stranger who interfered in the assemblies of the people was regarded as a traitor, and was punished by their laws with death. Had President Lincoln and General Schenck lived in the time of the free commonwealth of Athens, and interfered with the assemblies of the people as they did with the right of free suffrage in Maryland, they would have been executed as traitors and felons, and would have justly deserved their fate. Yes, sir, in that free commonwealth, under their laws, had such an interference taken place as has been proved incontestably by the evidence I have read to have taken place in Maryland, he who did it would have been punished with death as a traitor: and yet we find the Senate, through one of its committees, reporting against the passage of a bill visiting a much milder punishment than death upon those who interfere to prevent free elections, and that, too, upon the ground, as they state in their report, that the elections, have been fair! They say there is no ground for the complaint that anybody entitled to vote was prevented from voting, or that there was any interference in the election, when the facts stand out so prominently that none can deny or dispute but that the interference was most atrocious, flagrant, and outrageous.

General Schenck commenced his operations to crush out freedom of elections, and to prevent political organization against the Administration before he issued his order, No. 53, dated October 28, 1863. From the public journals I see that early in the fall of 1863, the Democrats of Talbot county, on the Eastern Shore, held a convention and nominated candidates for local offices of their county, clerk, sheriff, &c. The officers of the convention, and some of the parties named as candidates, gentlemen of the highest character and respectability, were arrested and required to report at headquarters in Baltimore, where General

Schenck required them to take the following oath, which is cut from the Easton Gazette, Maryland.

"RELEASED FROM ARREST.—The Easton (Maryland) Gazette states that the parties recently arrested in that town while attending a political convention have been released after subscribing to the following:

"'We, the subscribers, do hereby pledge ourselves and obligate by this written agreement that we will not, during the present rebellion against the Government and authority of the United States, organize or assist in the organization of any party inimical or opposed to the Administration of said Government; that we will not nominate, assist in the nomination; nor vote for any candidate or candidates for office of district, county, State, or General Government who are in sympathy with the so-called confederate States government, or opposed to the rigorous prosecution of the war now waged for the complete suppression of the existing rebellion. All this we promise and pledge without any mental reservation whatever, with a full purpose to keep and observe the same.'"

General Schenck required these gentlemen to swear that they would not during the present rebellion organize or assist in the organization of any party inimical or opposed to the Administration. Was there ever a more outrageous assault upon the rights of the citizen? General Schenck's object seems to have been to crush out all political opposition to his chief, Abraham Lincoln.

I honor the profession of arms; it is a noble profession. The brave soldier who fights the battles of his country, who draws his sword in in defense of the honor, constitution, and laws of his country, and in defense of the liberties of the people, is justly entitled to and will receive our confidence, admiration, and warmest gratitude—all honor to such noble warriors! But he who holds position in the army of his country and uses his power to overthrow the constitution and laws of his country, to strike down the liberties of the people, to prevent free ballot and to build up the fortunes of a political party, as has been done in Maryland, will receive the scorn and contempt of all good, wise, and patriotic men.

INTERFERENCE IN DELAWARE.

The committee in their report treat briefly of the elections in the State of Delaware. I will not enter at any great length into a discussion as to the mode of conducting the election in Delaware. It have here a report of a committee of the Legislature of that State in which they examine fully into that whole question. The sworn proof is in the volume I now hold in my hand. It is proved incontestably that the elections in Delaware in 1862 were carried to a great degree by the interference of the military. Governor Cannon—the Governor whom the Committee on Military Affairs laud in their report because in a proclamation to the people of that State he enjoins all good citizens and civil officers of that State to obey the military order General Schenck had issued concerning elections in Delaware, and they contrast his conduct with that of the Governor of Maryland. Mr. Cannon, it appears from the report and evidence, was elected Governor of Delaware in consequence of military interference. It is very clearly shown in the report of the committee' of the Legislature of Delaware that the military did interfere, and that they did it at the instance of Mr. Cannon, who was then a candidate for Governor, and other candidates' for high positions. It is also proved in the report that at what they call the "little election" in Delaware, which occurs about a month before the general election, the Democrats indicated' a strength that would carry the State by a large vote, and the Republican leaders had the military brought in to prevent their defeat at the general election. It is proven by some of these provost marshals, and the provost marshals were in chief command, it seems, in Delaware, that they did not think that there was any necessity for the military being there to preserve order. A singular fact in connection with these Delaware elections is, that these provost marshals were commissioned by the Secretary of War, Mr. Stanton, on the very eve of the election. The commissions were received the day before the election and were sent to Delaware in blank, and were there filled up by the party leaders of the Republican party.

It is further shown that great interferences took place in the election there. It is further proven that the then Governor of Delaware did not ask the intervention of the military to prevent domestic disorder and violence; but that he was opposed to their coming. The testimony of the ex-Governor is embodied in the report. It is proved very clearly by the testimony of ex-Governor Ross, that General Wool, a major general in the army of the United States, came to the State of Delaware with a body of troops on the eve of the election. General Wool, in an interview which Governor Ross had with him, told him the election should be fair. After the polls were opened, discovering that these provost marshals and their adherents were preventing the Democrats from casting their votes, and interfering with the election, Governor Ross went to General Wool and told him he promised them a fair election, and the provost marshals were conducting it far otherwise than fairly. General Wool told him—and it is in the testimony of Governor Ross, sworn to in this book—that for the time being he had no control; that he was really under the command of the provost marshals, and declined to interpose in order to prevent interference at the polls.

Thus it will be seen that Mr. Stanton, the Secretary of War, was engaged in this business of interfering in elections. He sent blank commissions of provost marshals to his party friends to be filled up to suit their purposes. Sir, they must have been very menial tools of power to consent to act as provost marshals to do this dirty work of preventing honest and loyal men from casting their votes It seems it was all trusted to the members of the Republican party who were managing for the time and controlling the election. You will find that the President put his own hand to the work in Maryland, aided by General Schenck; General Burnside of infamous memory controls it in Kentucky;

and Edwin M. Stanton, the Secretary of War, perpetrates a similar outrage in Delaware.

I discovered from the reading of the testimony that instructions accompanied the commissions of these provost marshals; and I introduced a resolution into the Senate asking the Secretary of War to send us the orders and the instructions, if any had been given, to those provost marshals. That has been some three weeks ago. A few days ago I had a second resolution sent to the Secretary of War on the subject; and he stands in contempt of the Senate and does not send us those instructions and orders to his provost marshals, or tell us whether he ever sent any or not; and yet one of the provost marshals swears that instructions did accompany his commission, and he exhibited his commission from Mr. Stanton as Secretary of War.

INTERFERENCE IN MISSOURI.

So far as the Missouri elections are concerned, it is unnecessary for me to say much. I must do the military commander of Missouri the justice to say that of all the orders that have been issued on the subject in the States, his are by far the best; and yet there are one or two things in his orders that are very objectionable. I repeat, however, that it is unnecessary for me to say much in regard to the Missouri elections. I have before me and I have examined the testimony taken in three contested seats in the other end of this Capitol from that State, and I can say without fear of contradiction there never were greater outrages committed on the elective franchise than by the military in Missouri. Why, sir, they arrested and imprisoned men for attempting to vote, they tore up the poll-books, they drove legal voters from the election poll, and almost every outrage you could imagine, they committed. Upon that subject we have sworn testimony, and that testimony is undergoing investigation in the other end of this Capitol; and I find by the journals of yesterday morning that the Committee of Elections in the House have determined to send back all those cases to the people upon the sole ground that the military interfered with the freedom of the elections. It is a pregnant fact, and one that I hope the Senate will consider on the passage of this bill. When we find such evidence and such action upon the evidence as has taken place in the other House, I do not think the Senate ought for a moment to hesitate to pass this bill, on the ground that there has been no interference with elections.

MILITARY USURPATIONS — AMNESTY PROCLAMATION, &c.

But, Mr. President, had there been no such interference, it would still be wise and proper to pass this bill. We should not wait for crime to be committed before we pass laws denouncing penalties against it; but as wise lawgivers we should make the law to prevent as well as punish crime. The fact that the law was on the statute-book would deter those who contemplated such offenses. If such offenses should be committed as are set forth in this bill, none will say that the offenders ought not to be severely punished. The evidence is full and abundant that there has been the most outrageous interference by the military in four of the States of this Union in the elections.

The writer of the report from the Military Committee claims power to do all those things under the law of necessity, military necessity, and it is under that plea that these persons are justified. I have heard that plea, Mr. President, ever since these encroachments upon the Constitution and the laws of the country have been going on. They speak of the nation struggling for its life. Well, sir, I confess, and I do it regrettingly, too, that the nation is struggling for its life. I regard the Constitution and the laws made in pursuance thereof as the life of the country, and that is seriously endangered, for we find the President and those he controls, who should protect and defend the Constitution, invading it at almost every point. I do not think that the life of the nation is in any more danger from the rebels—though God knows that danger is great enough—than it is from domestic traitors at home, who are charged with the preservation of the Constitution and yet are killing it.

The writer of the report seems to assume that the Executive has a right to govern every other department of the Government, and control the institutions of all the States, and that he is to be appealed to for the protection of the people. Is it not most humiliating, sir, that the people in a country governed by constitutions and laws should be driven to appeal to any man for protection? Montesquieu, in his book upon the Rise and Fall of the Roman Empire, makes a remark on this subject which I will read to the Senate. Speaking of the Senate's entreating Pompey to undertake the defense of the republic, he says:

"If that name might be properly given to a government which implored protection from one of its citizens."

The doctrine of those gentlemen who desire to clothe the Executive with this supreme power, with this absolute power, with this more than dictatorial power, places this great Republic in that humiliating attitude. I do not think that a citizen in a country governed by law was ever driven to the necessity of appealing to one man for protection. Sir, the citizen who for the time being fills the Chief Executive office is bound to see that the laws are faithfully executed; that is his duty. There is no liberty save in the supremacy of the law. In all free governments the citizen appeals to the law for protection.

Mr. President, all usurpers and all tyrants that have gone before us, those who have overthrown the liberties of every people who have lost their liberties, claim their powers under this plea of necessity. Cæsar, when he led his army from Gaul, crossed the Rubicon, and overthrew the liberties of his country, did it upon the plea of necessity, and tyrants the world over have done the same thing. The President seems to me to follow in the footsteps of Cæsar, Pompey, and Cromwell. The Chief Magistrate, I regret to say, seems to copy all the faults, while he has exhibited none of the virtues of those distinguished men.

Now, sir, allow me to read to you what the same writer says about the action of these two distinguished men in Rome—how it was they sapped the foundations of the liberties of the people. Speaking of Pompey, Montesquieu says:

"He employed the vilest of the populace to incommode the magistrates in the exercise of their functions, in hopes that wise people, growing weary of living in a state of anarchy, would be urged by despair to create him dictator."

Do we not find the same thing going on here? Is not the President and his military officers interfering with the civil magistrates? There can be no doubt about it.

Speaking of Cæsar, the same author says:

"He raised troubles in the city by his emissaries; he made himself master of all elections; and consuls, prætors, and tribunes purchased their promotions at their own price."

"He made himself master of all elections." That is what is being done here. How was it with Oliver Cromwell? The Protector appointed twelve major generals to take charge of the twelve districts into which he divided the British empire, and they went forth armed with all power; they decimated the people; they taxed them at their discretion, and exacted enormous tribute from them, and in that way the people were held in subservience to the military authority. The Protector dissolved one Parliament, and carried on his government by a Council of State. After a while, believing that such had been the glory of his administration in its foreign wars, and such was the subserviency of the people created by the action of his twelve major generals, that he could have a Parliament elected that would be subservient to his will, he ordered an election. The election was held, and how was it conducted? I will read an extract from Hume on that subject:

"Cromwell began to hope that, by his administration attended with so much luster and success abroad, so much order and tranquillity at home, he had now acquired such authority as would enable him to meet the representatives of the nation, and would assure him of their dutiful compliance with his government. He summoned a Parliament; but not trusting altogether to the good-will of the people, he used every art which his new model of representation allowed him to employ, in order to influence the elections and fill the House with his own creatures. Ireland, being entirely in the hands of the army, chose few but such officers as were most acceptable to him. Scotland showed a like compliance; and as the nobility and gentry of that kingdom regarded their attendance on English Parliaments as an ignominious badge of slavery, it was on that account more easy for the officers to prevail in the elections. Notwithstanding all these precautions, the Protector still found that the majority would not be favorable to him. He set guards, therefore, on the door, who permitted none to enter but such as produced a warrant from his Council; and the Council rejected about a hundred, who either refused a recognition of the Protector's government, or were on other accounts obnoxious to him. These protested against so egregious a violence, subversive of all liberty; but every application for redress was neglected, both by the Council and the Parliament.

"The majority of the Parliament, by means of these arts and violences, was now at least either friendly to the Protector, or resolved, by their compliance, to adjust, if possible, their military government to their laws and liberties."

Mr. President, from the authorities I have read it seems that we are following in the footsteps of nations whose liberties have been overthrown and trampled down beneath the iron heel of military despotism. It is said that history but re-enacts itself, and it seems to me, in view of all the lights in the past which we have before us, that this once great and glorious country of ours is about to be destroyed and its liberties overthrown by the same means that have destroyed all free governments that have gone before us. It is a fact that we should well ponder and consider, that it is by military power that free nations, heretofore have lost their liberties. It is our duty, if it is possible to do so by wise laws, to see to it that the hopes of the world in regard to the glory, prosperity, and perpetuity of this Republic shall not be wrecked on the same rock.

I said a moment ago that if we are to have liberty we must be governed by law; that liberty can only exist in the supremacy of the law. On that point Mr. Locke says:

"Where law ends tyranny begins. If the law be transgressed to another's harm, him whomsoever in authority exceeds the power given him by the law, and makes use of the force he has under his command to compass that upon the subject which the law allows not, ceases in that to be a magistrate, and acting without authority may be opposed as any other man who invades the rights of another."

That is a wise maxim laid down by Mr. Locke, but if I had uttered it a year or two ago my loyalty, perhaps, would have been very much questioned. The President of the United States, however, utters the same sentiment in his inaugural address, for in that address he declares:

"If by the mere force of numbers a majority should deprive a minority of any clearly written constitutional right, it might in a moral point of view justify revolution; certainly would if the lost right were a vital one."

The last part of the extract I read from Mr. Locke is in substance the same. He says if the lawful rights of the people are overthrown by their magistrates, they have a right to resist. Mr. Lincoln says the violation of the Constitution in a vital point would justify revolution; and allow me to tell you, Senators, that one reason why the people have submitted so quietly, so uncomplainingly, to the many usurpations of the Executive is that they hoped in a short time to have the privilege of relieving themselves of the President by means of free suffrage; but if you allow the military to prevent free elections you not only stab the Republic in its very vitals but you will by that means cause many persons who think that these usurpations of power ought to be resisted only at the ballot-box to look about for other means to redress their grievances. If you do not wish blood to flow in this land, if you wish to preserve our institutions, allow the people the privilege of turning out every four years their President if they desire to do so. Give them free speech, free press, free suffrage. Allow me to tell you that these three things are the greatest conservative elements in this country. The people will bear patiently great wrongs from wicked and corrupt officials, provided free speech, free press, and free suffrage are left them. By these lawful agencies they can in a short time turn unworthy and corrupt officials from their high places. A wise and prudent people prefer the use of these constitutional and peaceful agencies to force to rid themselves of unworthy public servants. In the various phases of political parties that have existed heretofore in this country, the Executive has been sometimes denounced for usurpation, and we have had no revolutions; and why? Because the people knew that they had the power in their hands, if a majority were of their opinion, in a short time to clothe other magistrates with power. But, sir, for the first time in the history of the Republic we find that the Federal military have taken charge of elections. It is a matter that the Senate should gravely consider and prevent, if they possibly can do so, by placing upon the statute-book salutary and wise laws to prevent the recurrence of the evil. Senators, if you allow the President to exercise this power, if that magistrate should be a corruptor an ambitious or a depraved man, do you not know that he will use it for the purpose of perpetuating his power, and re-electing himself? There is no Senator in this Chamber but must know that what I say is true. Why not, then, pass the bill without hesitation, and do your duty at least to prevent it?

I regret to say that I am very thoroughly satisfied that the President is using the military in this way, and tampering with elections for the purpose of perpetuating his power. Nothing will convince me to the contrary but such action on the part of the Executive as will clearly indicate that he is not using the military arm of the Government for that purpose. His amnesty proclamation is a move in that direction; and at this point I will for a few moments, advert to that proclamation, dated the 8th December last, accompanying the President's last message. I regard the proclamation as unwise, inexpedient, unconstitutional, and revolutionary. I do not know that I have ever seen a more revolutionary document than this proclamation. It is revolutionary because it overthrows the Constitution, overthrows the laws, and by it the Executive assumes powers that are not conferred upon him by the Constitution. In a word, he sets up his own will as the law; he becomes for the time being a despot; his will governs instead of the Constitution and the written laws of the country. The President, in his proclamation, not only prescribes the qualifications of voters, but the qualifications of officers. What right has the President of the United States, whence does he derive the power, to say, who shall be a qualified elector in the State of Arkansas, or who shall be qualified to hold office in that State? Take his proclamation and his letter to General Steele, and you will see that the President assumes all these powers. He undertakes to prescribe the qualification of voters, and of the persons who shall hold office in that State. I read yesterday and commented upon the clause of the Constitution that declares who are qualified electors. I suppose no Senator will contend that the President of the United States, by virtue of his office, has the right to alter or to amend the constitutions of the States of this Union, or the right to say who shall be a qualified voter for the State officers in any State, or who shall be qualified to hold State offices; and yet the President assumes the power to do all these things in his amnesty proclamation and in his letter to General Steele touching elections in the State of Arkansas. I will read from that letter on this matter:

"The constitution and laws of the State, as before the rebellion, are in full force, except that the constitution is so modified as to declare that there shall be neither slavery nor involuntary servitude except in the punishment of crime."

By what authority does the President of the United States assume to amend the constitution of the State of Arkansas? I had thought that that right was conferred alone upon the sovereign people of that State. I have always supposed that under our form of Government the people, and the people alone, were clothed with the sovereign power to make constitutions and to alter or amend them. And yet we find that the President of the United States undertakes to exercise that power. It is a power as despotic and as absolute as that exercised by William of Normandy in England after the battle of Hastings. Is there a Senator here who will dare rise in his place and say that the President has the power to alter or amend the constitution of any State of the Union? The President assumes it in his letter to General Steele, and he undertakes in the amnesty proclamation to prescribe the qualifications of voters, for he says that all who choose to come in and take that oath may exercise the right of citizens. In this letter to General Steele he requires that when the officers are elected they shall appear at General Steele's headquarters at Little Rock and take that oath. Of course that is prescribing the qualification of the officers as well as of the electors.

That is not all, Mr. President, that is being done in this direction. We find that the same thing, to some extent, is being done in Tennessee; Governor Johnson's proclamation, although very objectionable, is free from many of the objections that are contained in the others. General Banks is commanding in Louisiana, and he issues orders regulating elections, regulating labor, and establishing a kind of semi-peonage among the negroes, and in his order he uses this remarkable language:

"Opinion is free and candidates are numerous. Open hostilities cannot be permitted. Indifference will be treated as a crime and faction is treason."

Was there ever so atrocious a sentiment as that? Here is a major general of the Army of the United States who speaks of candidates being numerous and opinions free, and yet he says, in the very next two lines, that he will treat indifference as a crime; in plain Saxon, that the man who does not vote will be a criminal and will be punished with an iron hand. What kind of freedom of opinion is that? Yet, sir, we find one of the President's creatures, one of his military subordinates, whom he has put over one of the military departments, uttering that unconstitutional and atrocious sentiment.

You see, sir, that the military are swallowing up all the other powers of the Government, both State and national; and it seems that those who attempt to pass laws to arrest it meet with very little favor from the Committee on Military Affairs. I hope we shall fare better in the Senate. The proclamation of the President is unjust to loyal men. That proclamation will not allow any person to exercise the functions of citizenship in one of those States unless he shall take the oath prescribed. Then, and only then, is he a qualified voter. Only then is he qualified to hold office. And who are allowed to avail themselves of the benefits of this amnesty? Any person, a citizen of one of those States, can avail himself of it unless he falls within the excepted classes; and those are, officers in the army of high grade, such as have left the Congress of the United States, &c. It is unnecessary for me to enumerate them all. The exception applies to those who have held civil office and those who have held high military command, &c. All others who come in and take this oath are clothed by the grace of the President's pardoning power with the qualifications of suffrage and they are permitted to hold office.

I say it is unjust to loyal men. There are many staunch, loyal men in those States, men who never have had sympathy with the rebellion. The President, in his first message, said that in all those States, except South Carolina, he believed a majority were loyal to the old Union. The President requires all these persons to take this oath. If a man had been in the army of the confederate States, and had slaughtered a hundred Union soldiers, he is a qualified elector on coming and taking this oath; but a man who had ever been a Union man, but who could not conscientiously take the oath, is excluded. I hold that the oath is of such a character that a conscientious, honest man would not take it; and moreover I think it very unjust to require of a man who is and has ever been devoted to the institutions of his country, and who has been in nowise engaged in this rebellion, to submit to the humiliating condition prescribed for those whom the President regards as pardoned felons.

The oath requires a man to swear that he will support the Constitution of the United States. I suppose with all Union men there would be no difficulty about that part of the oath, for they have been supporting it all the time. But it further requires them to support the negro policy of the President and his proclamation on that subject. I, for one, firmly believe that the President's emancipation proclamation is unconstitutional. I think he had no power to issue it or to proclaim the freedom of negroes in the States; and I have no doubt that a large majority of the Union men in that country concur with me in opinion. Yet, sir, you see he requires them to take that oath, which an honest loyal man cannot take, if he believed his proclamation to be in violation of the Constitution; when he swears to support the Constitution, he cannot in the same oath swear to support proclamations which deprive him of his property, and which he thinks are in conflict with the Constitution.

The oath requires a man not only to swear to support the proclamations that have been issued, but to swear to support those that may be issued in the future. It applies as well to the future as to the past or the present. What honest man would swear that he would support all other proclamations the President might make on the subject of negroes or negro slavery, even provided he approved the proclamations already issued? The President, in the plenitude of his power, might issue a proclamation that only negroes should vote, and that only negroes should hold office; and yet he would swear a man in advance to support it. I tell you, sir, an honest, conscientious man cannot take this oath. This proclamation and the oath elevates the negro above the white man. I will read one clause of it on that subject. Speaking of those who are excluded from the benefit of the proclamation, the President says:

"And all who have engaged in any way in treating colored and white persons in charge of such otherwise than lawfully as prisoners of war, and which persons may have been found in the United States service as soldiers, seamen, or in any other capacity."

He excludes from this amnesty a soldier in the rebel army, if he has treated a negro soldier, seaman, or white persons in charge of such, otherwise than as a prisoner of war; but he does not exclude those engaged in the confederate army who have treated white soldiers and white seamen or their commanders otherwise than as prisoners of war. If one of those rebel soldiers lays his hand on a negro, and does not treat him as a prisoner of war, he cannot be pardoned; but he may take white soldiers and seamen prisoners and execute them in cold blood after they have surrendered; he may treat them with the utmost cruelty and with the most savage barbarity, and that man can come up and avail himself of the amnesty in President Lincoln's proclamation. If he touches the saintly person of a negro in that way, there is no chance for him to avail himself of the President's amnesty.

I believe that this is a Government of white men. I believe it was made by white men and for the benefit of white men; and I still believe that a white man is better than a negro. I think every such discrimination in favor of the negro against the people of our own race is most atrocious, and wholly unjustifiable.

There is another thing in this amnesty proclamation upon which I will say a word: and that is the one-tenth principle. When one tenth of the population, that is one tenth of those who voted at the last presidential election, shall come forward and take the oath, they shall be enough to govern, says the President. That destroys every principle of republican Government. It is a principle that I suppose none will deny in a republican and democratic Government that majorities shall rule; but here the President says one tenth may rule. He overthrows the great principle upon which all republican and democratic Governments rest, and he says one tenth, and that one tenth may be, and I have no doubt will be, composed of the most despicable people of that country; for it is that kind who are willing to come in, after they have been engaged in the rebel army, if they get a little tired, and swear out of it. I have not much opinion of those men who swear into one army one day and into another the next. They are not the kind of men who should be permitted to govern any people.

The loyal men there who believe the President's negro policy is unconstitutional cannot, avail themselves of the amnesty. It is such only as will come up and submit themselves to that humiliating degradation; brave and upright men are not going to humiliate themselves by taking such a degrading oath. One tenth of that kind of men are to govern. They are to govern the nine tenths. How will they govern them? He promises them that protection which is provided for by the Constitution, which declares "the United States shall guaranty to every State in the Union a republican form of Government." I suppose the President intends to keep charge of the governments of these States in all time by a standing army to enable this one tenth to govern the nine tenths. Sir, you cannot cause one tenth of any free white people on this continent to govern nine tenths, unless you make the nine tenths absolute slaves. You must stand by with your bayonets fixed and coerce nine tenths into absolute unconditional obedience before one tenth can govern them. The government the President proposes to guaranty to these States is not a republican government within the meaning of the Constitution, and it is a gross abuse of language to call it so.

Many honorable Senators on the other side of the Chamber, and the school of politicians to which the President belongs, have made a great deal of clamor about the three-fifths slave representation provided for in the Constitution. Carry out this one-tenth principle in Arkansas, the one-tenth who will avail themselves of the amnesty of the President, by taking that most humiliating of oaths, will have it in their power to elect all the members of Congress to which Arkansas would be entitled upon the enumeration of her population at the last census; and do you not think that one man down there will have as much power as ten men in Minnesota or Michigan? Certainly so; and that is the policy of the President whose party has been clamorous upon the negro representation and three-fifths provided for in the Constitution for the slave States.

Sir, I do not care upon what ground you place the question; the President is not clothed with the power that he has exercised. There are two theories among the Republicans on this question. Some say these States are dead, out of the Union, have committed suicide; others say they are still States in the Union. Well, if they are States in the Union, what power has the President of the United States to alter or amend their constitutions, or to fix the qualification of State officers? He has none. Nobody will contend that the President of the United

States, by virtue of his office, has any power or any right to alter or amend the constitution of any State in the Union. If Arkansas is a State in the Union the President has no power to alter its constitution, which he has assumed to do. If it is not a State of the Union, but is a territory that has been acquired by conquest, purchase, or otherwise, then I ask what authority has the President to admit it as a State into the Union, or to make a constitution for it? Is it not plainly written in the Constitution that Congress may admit new States? Congress and Congress alone has the power to form governments for the Territories of the United States. If he holds, then, this to be a Territory, he exercises a power conferred by the Constitution on Congress. So take it in any way you please, and the President is excising power absolutely forbidden by the Constitution.

I regard the amnesty proclamation as a most unfortunate one. I believe it will put off and delay a cessation of hostilities, and perhaps a reconstruction of the Union, for a long time to come. I admit that the President is clothed with the pardoning power; but when he undertook to issue an amnesty proclamation he should have made that proclamation ample, full, complete; he should have restored these people to all their rights of person and property under the Constitution; he should have told all those who came back and rallied under the old flag that they should enjoy all the rights and all the protection that the Constitution secures to a citizen of the United States. By such a proclamation the President would have weakened the rebel cause. I believe that if such a proclamation were now issued Arkansas and many of the border States of the confederacy would soon return to the Union.

As it is, you place upon them the most humiliating conditions, conditions that a brave and honest people who love liberty never, never will submit to. Why, sir, is there a Senator here who would, for the purpose of being permitted to exercise the right of citizenship in a democratic and republican Government, take an oath that he would be bound to support all the proclamations that the Executive should issue on any one given subject? No, sir. The whole scheme of the President is impracticable. The object, in my judgment, is not to bring those States back into the Union in good faith, but to establish a kind of rotten-borough system, to have votes to help to re-elect him President. We may as well speak plainly as we are speaking on the subject. I believe the expedition sent down to Florida was for the purpose of inaugurating the same system there; and that foolish and disastrous expedition results about this way: a loss of fifteen hundred of the soldiers of the United States in an effort to get three electoral votes.

I stated a moment ago that the Executive was swallowing up every other department of the Government. I am not going to consume the time of the Senate by reciting at any great length the usurpations of the Administration.

The President and the party in power have violated the Constitution in almost every vital part. The Constitution confers on Congress the power to raise and support armies, and to provide and to maintain a Navy. The President has added to the regular Army twenty thousand men without warrant of law. He has added eighteen thousand seamen to the Navy without the authority of law. The Constitution has been violated by taking money from the Treasury without authority of law.

" *The freedom of speech* has been violated by the arrest and imprisonment of a number of persons, charged with no crime, and whose only offense was the utterance of sentiments distasteful to the men in power.

" *The freedom of the press* has been subverted by the suppression of a number of newspapers.

" *The right to security from arrest when no crime is charged* has been disregarded in the arrest and incarceration of a large number of persons, denounced by the parasites of the Administration as 'sympathizers with the rebellion.'

" *The right to security from unlawful searches and seizures* has been violated in numerous instances, in which domiciles have been visited, and papers, &c., seized without legal authority.

" *The right of a trial by jury* has been refused in the cases of citizens arrested and imprisoned, or banished by military orders of courts-martial.

" The freedom of every citizen has been taken from him by the illegal and unnecessary suspension of the right to demand the writ of *habeas corpus*.

" *The right of the property* has been abrogated by the emancipation proclamation and the confiscation act.

" The inviolability of contracts has been destroyed by the act which makes depreciated Treasury notes a *legal tender* for all debts.

" *The freedom of religious worship* has been violated on repeated occasions by the interference of military officers.

" *The right of States to the management of their militia* has been taken from them by the conscription act, which places the whole military power of the country at the disposal of the President.

" *The formation of the State of West Virginia* was a violation of the third section of the fourth article of the Constitution.

" *The heretofore undisputed right of the people to elect their legislators and rulers* has been taken from them, and the will of majorities disregarded, as is abundantly manifested in the manner in which elections have recently been carried by the grossest corruption, by military orders, in the border States of the South.

Nearly all the violations of the Constitution that I have enumerated have been by the Executive Department of the Government. It seems to me that the Executive, aided by the military power, has swallowed up the powers of this Government, both State and national, almost as completely as the rod of Aaron swallowed up the rods of the magicians.

We are all subject at any day to arrest and imprisonment without warrant, without trial, without a hearing. We find the President, through his Secretaries and military commanders, exercising that power. I regard the presidential office as a unit, and that all those Secretaries act by virtue of his authority. They are but his chief clerks, as Mr. Randolph used to call them, and the present Secretary of State, in one of his dispatches to some Government in Europe, says it is all the action of the President, whether done by one of the Departments or another. That is certainly the true theory of the Government. Citizens of the highest position and respectability have been arrested without warrant and thrown into prison, where they have languished, some of them, as long as seventeen months without accusation or trial. These officials go on as if they would enjoy power forever. This is an exercise of power that would have caused a dictator of Rome to be punished. Cicero, during his consulship, when he was engaged in putting down the conspiracy of Catiline, being clothed with dictatorial power by the Roman Senate, put to death five Roman citizens, and that, too, with the advice and consent of the Senate. For overthrowing that conspiracy no man ever was more lauded, and for that he was called parens patriæ; but after that struggle was over, Cicero, who had been so eulogized by all Rome, was indicted, tried, convicted, and banished because he had put a Roman citizen to death without trial. Yes, sir, with a written Constitution that absolutely forbids it, when there is no authority in our Government to confer dictatorial power upon the President, he imprisons at will thousands of our citizens without charge, without trial. Sir, the President and his satraps had better beware. A brave people will not stand these things always. A day of reckoning will come, and an awful day it will be to those guilty men who have overthrown and trodden under foot the Constitution and laws of their country, and unlawfully deprived the people of their dearest rights.

It is pleasant when we see that a gleam of light has broken in upon persons from whom we expected little good. I hold in my hands an extract from a speech of the most distinguished radical in America—a man of learning, a man of eloquence, indeed of rare elocution. I had thought that his whole soul was fully absorbed in this negro question, and that he could not talk without bringing it in. I mean Wendell Phillips. But while I think him a fanatic of the deepest dye, he differs from others of his party; he sometimes has lucid intervals. Allow me to read an extract from a speech of that eloquent man on this very point.

"But let me remind you of another tendency of the time. You know for instance, that the writ of habeas corpus by which Government is bound to render a reason to the judiciary before it lays its hands upon a citizen, has been called the high-water mark of English liberty. The present Napoleon, in his treatise on the English Constitution, calls it the germ of English institutions. Lieber says that that, with free meetings like this, and a free press, are the three elements which distinguish liberty from despotism, and all

that Saxon blood has gained in the battles and toils of two hundred years are these three things. Now, to-day, every one of those—habeas corpus, the right of free meeting, and free press, is annihilated in every square mile of the Republic. We live to-day, every one of us, under martial law or mob law. The Secretary of State puts into his bastile, with a warrant as responsible as that of Lewis, any man whom he pleases; and you know that neither press nor lips may venture to arraign the Government without being silenced. "We are tending with rapid strides—you say, inevitable; I don't deny it, necessarily; I don't question it; we are tending to that strong Government which frightened Jefferson; toward that unlimited debt, that endless army. We have already those alien and sedition laws which, in 1798, wrecked the Federal party and summoned the Democratic into existence. For the first time on the continent we have passports, which even Louis Bonaparte pronounced useless and odious. For the first time in our history, Government spies frequent our great cities."

That, sir, is a very graphic and truly eloquent picture of the times in which we are, and I hope the country will take warning. We seem to have yielded everything to the military power, and I regret to say with a tameness and submission which, in my judgment, are unbecoming members of an American Congress. A military republic we have, and we have a republic but in name—the animating principle, the security of the citizen in life, liberty, and property, is gone. Allow me to call attention to an extract on that subject from one of the speeches of the great Webster, who spoke upon that, as he did upon most other subjects, with the most profound wisdom. This is from his speech delivered on the completion of the Bunker Hill monument:

"A military republic, a Government founded on mock elections, and supported only by the sword, is a movement indeed, but a retrograde and disastrous movement from the regular and old-fashioned monarchical system. If men would enjoy the blessings of republican Government they must govern themselves by reason, by mutual counsel, and consultation, by a sense and feeling of general interest, and by the acquiescence of the minority in the will of the majority, properly expressed; and above all, the military must be kept, according to the language of our Bill of Rights, in strict subordination to the civil authority. Whenever this lesson is not both learned and practiced, there can be no political freedom. Absurd, preposterous is it, a scoff and a satire on free forms of constitutional liberty, for forms of Government to be prescribed by military leaders, and the right of suffrage to be exercised at the point of the sword."

Sir, we are in those very times; we have seen the right of suffrage exercised at the point of the sword. There never was a time, it does not exist now, and has not existed since this unfortunate civil war commenced, in which it was necessary for the President to overthrow the Constitution and elevate the military above the civil power. There is power enough in the Constitution to furnish the President every dollar every man needed for this war. Congress can give him the sword and the purse. What more can you confer? Nothing. Where, then, the necessity and the excuse for these wanton violations of the Constitution, this reckless overthrow of the liberties of the people, this setting at naught the laws and the constitutions of the States, the regulating of elections by the sword? None. None. The genius of our Government is founded upon the principle that the military shall be kept in strict subordination to the civil power. But the friends of the President claim it as a matter of necessity to save the life of the nation, when they must see that the President is trampling under his feet the Constitution, and crushing out the liberties of the people, and destroying every vital principle that gives value to free Government.

But, sir, we have had other great chieftains before. There was a man who lived in this Republic that I suppose was thought by all wise and good men to be almost as great as Abraham Lincoln is thought to be by his cringing, truckling, and obsequious followers; that man was George Washington. He led our armies through a seven years' war in most trying times, when the organization of the civil authority was very defective. It had none of the force, none of the power that we have now under our well and admirably adjusted Constitution; when there was great difficulty in procuring men for the army and money to defray the necessary expenses of the Government. Many of the States failing to furnish their quotas of men and money, there being no central controlling power, Congress had no means of enforcing its decrees upon the States. Surrounded by such embarrassments, Washington for seven years led the armies of the colonies until the war was brought to a successful and glorious close. Did Washington, during that long and arduous struggle in which the colonies were engaged, ever think it necessary to subordinate the civil to the military authority? No, sir; no. In L783, when he resigned his commission at Annapolis, he was addressed by Thomas Mifflin, President of the Continental Congress, as follows:

"You have conducted the great military contest with wisdom and fortitude, invariably regarding the rights of the civil power through all disasters and dangers."

This I regard as the highest and most deserved compliment that was ever bestowed upon mortal man.

Sir, I would that this vascillating, dissembling, weak, and I fear wicked and corrupt, man in the White House had been infused with the wisdom, virtue, and patriotism that animated the soul and prompted the actions of the great Washington in our revolutionary struggle. Washington and his compatriots were engaged in a struggle for civil liberty; the sword was used only to resist the encroachment of tyrants, and was subordinated to the civil power. The resistance was successful. They then laid broad, deep, and strong the foundation of civil and religious liberty. They proclaimed the Constitution as the fundamental law, and threw it as a strong and impenetrable shield around the rights of the States and the liberties of the people. The Executive is now using the sword which should only be directed against the armed enemies of the Republic for the sacrilegious purpose of suppressing free speech, free press, and free suffrage, and the overthrow of the Constitution, the rights of the States, and liberties of the people of the adhering States.

ATTORNEY GENERAL BATES AROUSED.

Amid the startling assumptions of the military power we find that one member of the Cabinet has recently woke up on this subject.

The polite and venerable Attorney General, Mr. Bates, is seized with dread apprehension because the military power is interfering with the civil authority. I congratulate the country that the first law officer of the Government has at last sounded the alarm on this momentous question. I will read a part of the letter of the honorable Attorney General on this subject; and I do it with profound satisfaction.

It seems that the military authority arrested a Judge Knapp at Santa Fe, in the territory of New Mexico, and imprisoned him and otherwise interrupted him in the discharge of his duties. He wrote a letter, and a very manly one it was, protesting against the interference of the military to the Attorney General. The Attorney General took the matter under consideration and conferred with his Excellency the President; and thereupon he wrote this note to Judge Knapp:

"Your letter of the 4th of August complaining of military arrests was slow in reaching me, and then such was the urgent and continued occupation of the President in the great affairs of the Government that I have not been able until now to fix his attention on the particular outrage on you, as your letter makes me believe it to be.

"There seems to be a general and a growing disposition of the military wherever stationed, to engross all power, and to treat the civil government with contumely, as if the object were to bring it into contempt.

"I have delivered my opinion very plainly to the President, and I have reason to hope that he, in the main, concurs with me in believing that these arbitrary proceedings ought to be suppressed."

I am delighted that even the Attorney General has been aroused on this subject, and I should have been further delighted if he had announced that the President concurred with him in opinion; but instead of that he says he hopes he does in the main concur.

Now, sir, what have we seen for the last two years? We have seen the military authority overthrowing the civil rights of citizens in every part of the country. We have seen citizens, neither engaged in the military nor naval service of the United States, seized and tried before drum-head courts-martial and punished, and some of them banished from their country. We have seen the military arrest judges who were faithful, loyal, and true men; for instance, Judge Duff, in the State of Illinois, when presiding in his court; Judge Constable, of the same State; and Judge Carmichael, of Maryland. Judge Duff was brought here a prisoner and lodged in the Old Capitol, and without any charge being brought against him was released. Judge Carmichael was subsequently imprisoned in Fort McHenry. The Attorney General stood by and saw all that, and he complained not. I am glad that the imprisonment of this judge in New Mexico has aroused the Attorney General from his slumbers. I am rather inclined to believe that the reason why the Attorney General is waking up now is that the military has laid its mailed hand upon a Republican judge; for this judge was appointed by Mr. Lincoln. When Judges Constable, Duff, and Carmichael, who are Democrats, were arrested, we did not hear a word from the Attorney General. However, I congratulate the country that the Attorney General has at last woke up. It is better late than never. I have no doubt, judging from the long time it has taken the Attorney General to come to the conclusion that the military is attempting to overthrow the civil power, that he will wait until the seventh angel spoken of in the Revelation of John shall appear with one foot upon the land and the other upon the sea, trumpet in hand, and with loud and shrill blast summon a guilty world to final judgment, before he will begin to think for a moment that judgment day is near at hand. [Laughter.]

But, sir, I am delighted to find that the Attorney General is seized with dire alarm and dread apprehension in consequence of the encroachments of the military upon the civil power. The usurpations on the part of the military must have been very great to have brought forth the earnest protest of the Attorney General, who has not only given an opinion to the President that he had a right to suspend the privilege of the writ of *habeas corpus*, but has justified the President, as far as I am advised, in all of his subsequent usurpations of power. So astounding have these abuses become that even Mr. Bates has made protest against them.

I hope soon to hear others who have been liegemen of the President making manly protest against his usurpations; and to hear their appeals to their countrymen, rallying them to the rescue of their down-trodden liberties and a violated Constitution.

STANTON AND BUTLER RUN THE CHURCHES.

The Secretary of War, by virtue of what authority I do not know, has undertaken to administer the churches. Yes, sir, Edwin M. Stanton and General Butler are making themselves kind of chief pontiffs, and are "running the churches," the one in the valley of the Mississippi and the other in Norfolk and Portsmouth. If the President had decided to appoint persons to regulate and supervise the churches, and to take the religion of the people under his control, I would have supposed he would have selected gentlemen distinguished for their charity, kindness, and benevolence; men of high moral tone, meek and gentle in their manners; men eminent for their piety and theological learning, whose lives were adorned with every Christian virtue, to have discharged this most responsible and delicate trust. The two persons who have unlawfully assumed the control of the churches have none of the qualifications that I have indicated. If the President had searched the entire country I do not believe he could have found two persons upon whom to confer this delicate trust more unsavory than Edwin M. Stanton and Benjamin F. Butler. In their manners and intercourse they are both heartless ruffians; they are strangers to kindness, gentleness, benevolence, and those elevated manly virtues that gracefully adorn the life of a Christian gentleman. But, sir, they have usurped the power to control the churches in the localities I have mentioned, in violation of the Constitution and

the rights of the people who own those houses of public worship.

There is a little curious history about this subject. I have here the order of the Secretary of War placing under the control of Bishop Ames all the churches of the departments of the Missouri, the Tennessee, and the Gulf, belonging to the Methodist Episcopal Church South. This is one of the most startling usurpations of the military power that has fallen under my notice. The Constitution secures religious freedom to the citizen explicitly. Where did the Secretary of War get the power to transfer all these churches to the control of Bishop Ames? Listen to this order:

WAR DEPARTMENT, ADJUTANT GENERAL'S OFFICE, WASHINGTON, *November* 30, 1863.

To the generals commanding the departments of the Missouri, the Tennessee, and the Gulf, and all generals and officers commanding armies, detachments, and corps, and posts, and all officers in the service of the United States in the above-mentioned departments:

You are hereby directed to place at the disposal of Rev. Bishop Ames all houses of worship belonging to the Methodist Episcopal Church South in which a loyal minister, who has been appointed by a loyal bishop of said church, does not now officiate.

It is a matter of great importance to the Government, in its efforts to restore tranquillity to the community and peace to the nation, that Christian ministers should, by example and precept, support and foster the loyal sentiment of the people.

Bishop Ames enjoys the entire confidence of this Department, and no doubt is entertained that all ministers who may be appointed by him will be entirely loyal. You are expected to give him all the aid, countenance, and support practicable in the execution of his important mission.

You are also authorized and directed to furnish Bishop Ames and his clerk with transportation and subsistence when it can be done without prejudice to the service, and will afford them courtesy, assistance, and protection.

By order of the Secretary of War:

E. D. TOWNSEND, *Assistant Adjutant General.*

Sir, the first article in the Amendments of the Constitution says:

"Congress shall make no law respecting an establishment of religion, or prohibiting the free exercise thereof."

The Secretary of War violated that provision of the Constitution when he assumed jurisdiction over these churches. By what authority does he assume to appoint indirectly, through Bishop Ames, ministers to all the churches in the three departments mentioned belonging to the people called the Methodist Episcopal Church South? Bishop Ames does not belong to that church himself. He belongs to the Methodist Episcopal Church North. The Methodist Episcopal Church North and the Methodist Episcopal Church South are two separate and distinct institutions. They divided, I believe, in May, 1845. Since then they have been separate and distinct ecclesiastical bodies. Mr. Stanton by this unauthorized and unconstitutional order has clothed Bishop Ames with the power to take possession of all those churches. The minister may be loyal, but if he happens to have been appointed by a disloyal bishop he must be kicked out. They did deliver a chapel in Memphis under that order to Bishop Ames. I have the order here, and I will read it:

HEADQUARTERS DEPARTMENT OF MEMPHIS,
December 23, 1863.

Rev. BISHOP AMES:

In obedience to the orders of the Secretary of War, dated Washington, November 30, 1863, a copy of which is here attached, I place at your disposal a "house of worship" known as "Wesley Chapel," in the city of Memphis, State of Tennessee, the said house being claimed as the property of the Methodist Episcopal Church South, and there being no loyal minister, appointed by a loyal bishop, now officiating in said house of worship.

I am, very respectfully, your obedient servant,
JAMES C. VEATCH,
Brigadier General.

Mr. Stanton's order is being executed. I understand that the minister who was turned out of that church is a most excellent man, a man who preached Christ and Him crucified, and never babbled politics in his pulpit or elsewhere. He was turned out by the order of Pontiff Stanton, through his instrument and nuncio, Bishop Ames. I desire to cast no reflection upon Bishop Ames. I am told he is a worthy man. His sense of justice must have been very much blunted when he undertook this ecclesiastical mission.

While this was going on, on the very day General Veatch wrote the order to deliver Wesley Chapel to Bishop Ames, what do we find? We find a letter dated on that very day, December, 23, 1863, written by the President of the United States, concerning a certain minister in St. Louis—Mr. McPheeters—in which the President said he knew nothing about these things, and then goes on to say:

"But I must add that the United States Government must not, as by this order, undertake to run the churches."

"We must not undertake to run the churches." says the President; and he goes on to say that the Government has nothing to do with them. The President seems to be profoundly ignorant of what his chief of the War Department is doing. I do not know that I can properly solve the contradictions growing out of the President's declarations and the acts of his Secretary of War and major general.

Before I pass to that point, however, let me state that General Butler has issued an order that the churches at Portsmouth and Norfolk shall be controlled by the provost marshals, that they shall appoint and displace ministers in the churches, make assessments, &c., subject to the approval of the commanding general. Yes, sir, Ben. Butler, the Haynau of America, he whose administration in New Orleans brought disgrace on our country, whose friends in the House of Representatives refused a few days ago to allow a resolution to pass asking for a committee to investigate his conduct, is discharging the functions of grand hierarch in those cities. The provost marshal may present the minister to the church, but it must be by the approval of General Butler.

While all this was going on, the President wrote the letter, an extract from which I have read. He seems to be profoundly ignorant on the subject. He says the Government must not run the churches. I can only solve that by one of two hypotheses. It may be that the Presi-

dent has got it into his head that he will run the churches, but is not exactly ready to say so, and is using Stanton and Butler as a kind of feelers, as pilot-fish, as some of the friends of General Fremont and General Hunter think they were used in regard to the emancipation proclamation. General Fremont issued an emancipation proclamation. General Hunter issued one, and General Phelps issued another. The President revoked all those proclamations, and presently he issued an emancipation proclamation himself. The friends of those parties sometimes say that the President permitted those proclamations to see which way the popular current was running, then revoked them; and when he found the whole radical party, the whole Republican party, pretty much concurred in that policy, then he ventured upon it himself. He may be using Stanton as a pilot-fish in this matter, running him ahead; and if he thinks the people will not revolt at it and it will not be exceedingly obnoxious, he may venture upon this measure. "To save the life of the nation he may find it necessary to unite Church and State." In the meantime his letter concerning Rev. Mr. McPheeters is thrown out as something to fall back on in the event running the churches should appear very unpopular. This may be the proper solution of this matter. I do not, however, think it is.

My opinion is that Stanton is doing this thing upon his own authority against the wishes and without the knowledge of the President. What, then, is the duty of the President, if that be the case? If Mr. Stanton willfully and knowingly acts contrary to the wishes of the President, or issues orders of the gravest importance, involving rights of the most delicate character, compelling people not to worship at all, or to worship under the ministry of a man whom they do not want—if Mr. Stanton does this without the approval of the Executive, what ought the Executive to do? He ought to dismiss him from office, and do it quickly and promptly. If he does not do it the country will come to the conclusion that he does not so much object to it after all, notwithstanding his assertion "that the Government must not undertake to run the churches."

Sir, this is a most shocking usurpation of the military power; and I think if I have the good fortune to get this bill through about elections, I shall introduce another one punishing Secretaries of War and officers of the Army who attempt to appoint ministers to churches.

Mr. President, what are we to do when we see such startling usurpations by the military authority? Does not our duty imperiously drive us to the point of passing the most rigid laws to prevent a repetition of such outrages? If we maintain our institutions at all, we must maintain free press, free speech, and free suffrage, and last, but not least, freedom of religion. You see that they have all been stricken down by the military power. We shall fall far short of our duty unless we make every law that we think is calculated to restrain them. The people, if they maintain this Government, must do it, as I have said, by maintaining free speech, free press, and free suffrage. They must do another thing. They must keep separate and distinct the various departments of this Government. They must not allow one department to encroach upon another, but each department must be kept within its own sphere. Then one is a check upon the other. We must never allow them to be consolidated.

We should not allow the executive to encroach upon the judicial or the legislative department. Neither should we allow the legislative or the judicial to encroach on each other, or the executive department. Our fathers decreed these separate departments for wise purposes; and you will-have no liberty unless they are kept independent of each other. In a word, you will have no liberty except in the supremacy of the laws. Liberty must be regulated by law. No man, because he may be clothed with executive, judicial, or legislative power, should be allowed to trample the laws under his feet. The higher the official the more guilty the criminal, if he violates the laws of the land, because of his sworn duty to see them faithfully administered or executed. I would punish a judge of the Supreme Court, or the President of the United States, or a Senator in Congress much more harshly for infracting a law than I would an unlettered man in the country, because they know their duty ; they err knowingly, wittingly and maliciously.

Mr. President, I beg the pardon of the Senate for trespassing upon their time so long. The only excuse I have is in the importance of the subject. I know that so important a bill as this, taking into consideration the circumstances by which we are surrounded, has not been before this Congress. It was met at the very outset with opposition. On introducing the bill I hoped and believed that every Senator would support it with alacrity and pleasure; but it met with opposition at the threshold, and against my earnest protest it was referred to the Committee on Military Affairs, a committee to which it certainly did not properly belong. After keeping it for a long time, the committee have reported it back adversely, accompanied by a report of fifty-two printed pages. I had to review all the testimony and to examine that report at length; and I could not get through with the subject and do it justice in less time than I have occupied. I hope, therefore, for the reason I have assigned, that the Senate will excuse me for the great length of time that I have trespassed on their patience.

APPENDIX.

I

Proclamation by the Governor.

COMMONWEALTH OF KENTUCKY,
EXECUTIVE DEPARTMENT.

For the information and guidance of all officers at the approaching election, I have caused to be herewith published an act of the Legislature of Kentucky, entitled "An act to amend chapter fifteen of the Revised Statutes, entitled ' Citizens, Expatriation, and Aliens.' "

The strict observance and enforcement of this, and all other laws of this State regulating elections, are earnestly enjoined and required, as being alike due to a faithful discharge of duty, to the purity of elective franchise, and to the sovereign will of the people of Kentucky, expressed through their Legislature.

Given under my hand as Governor of Kentucky, at Frankfort, this 10th day of July, 1863, and in the seventy-second year of the Commonwealth.

J. F. ROBINSON.

By the Governor :
D. C. WICKLIFFE, *Secretary of State.*

An act to amend chapter fifteen of the Revised Statutes entitled "Citizens, Expatriation, and Aliens."

Be it enacted by the General Assembly of the Commonwealth of Kentucky, That any citizen of this State who shall enter into the service of the so-called confederate States, in either a civil or military capacity, or into the service of the so-called provisional government of Kentucky, in either a civil or military capacity, or having heretofore entered such service of either the confederate States or provisional government, shall continue in such service after this act takes effect, or shall take up or continue in arms against the military forces of the United States or the State of Kentucky, or shall give voluntary aid and assistance to those in arms against said forces, shall be deemed to have expatriated himself, and shall no longer be a citizen of Kentucky, nor shall he again be a citizen, except by permission of the Legislature by a general or special statute.

SEC. 2. That whenever a person attempts or is called on to exercise any of the constitutional or legal rights and privileges belonging only to citizens of Kentucky, he may be required to negative on oath the expatriation provided in the first section of this act ; and upon his failure or refusal to do so, shall not be permitted to exercise any such right or privilege.

SEC. 3. This act to be of force in thirty days from and after its passage.

Passed and became a law, the objections of the Governor to the contrary notwithstanding, March 11, 1862.

The following is the affidavit which may be used to negative the expatriation provided in the first section of the above act, upon the failure or refusal to take which no one can run for an office or vote for a candidate. It is the duty of all election officers to require it.

" You, A B, do solemnly swear that since the 11th day of April, 1862, you have not entered into nor been in the service of the so-called confederate States, nor in the service of the provisional government of Kentucky, in either a civil or military capacity ; and you do further solemnly swear that since the said 11th day of April, 1862, you have not taken up or been in arms against the military forces of the United States or the military forces of the State of Kentucky ; and you do further solemnly swear that since the said 11th day of April, 1862, you have in no way, either directly or indirectly, given any voluntary aid or assistance to any person or persons who were in arms against the military forces of the State of Kentucky. So help you God."

[General Orders, No. 120.]

HEADQUARTERS DEPARTMENT OF THE OHIO,
CINCINNATI, OHIO, *July* 31, 1863.

Whereas the State of Kentucky is invaded by a rebel force, with the avowed intention of overawing the judges of elections, of intimidating the loyal voters, keeping them from the polls, and forcing the election of disloyal candidates at the election on the 3d of August ; and whereas the military power of the Government is the only force that can defeat this attempt, the State of Kentucky is hereby declared under martial law, and all military officers are commanded to aid the constituted authorities of the State in the support of the laws and of the purity of suffrage, as defined in the late proclamation of his Excellency Governor Robinson. As it is not the intention of the commanding general to interfere with the proper expression of public opinion, all discretion in the conduct of the election will be, as usual, in the hands of the legally appointed judges at the polls, who will be held strictly responsible that no disloyal person will be allowed to vote, and to this end the military power is ordered to give them its utmost support. The civil authority, civil courts, and business will not be suspended by this order. It is for the purpose only of protecting, if necessary, the rights of loyal citizens, and the freedom of election.

By command of Major General Burnside.

LEWIS RICHMOND, *A. A. G.*

General Hartsuff and Rebel Sympathizers.

[General Orders, No. 14.]

No. 4.] HEADQUARTERS TWENTY-THIRD ARMY CORPS,
LEXINGTON, KENTUCKY, *July* 24, 1863.

For the information and guidance of officers in impressing property, it is hereby directed that, whenever its impressment may become necessary for the troops of the twenty-third Army Corps, it will be taken exclusively from rebels and rebel sympathizers ; and so long as the property needed is to be found belonging or pertaining to either of the above-named classes, no man of undoubted loyalty will be molested.

Among rebel sympathizers will be classed those persons in Kentucky, nominally Union men, but opposed to the Government and to the prosecution of the war, whose acts and words alike hinder the speedy and proper termination of the rebellion.

Property will only be taken by the proper staff officers, who will in every case give receipts for it. Appropriate blank receipts will be furnished by the chief commissary and chief quartermaster at these headquarters.

By command of Major General Hartsuff.

GEORGE B. DRAKE, *A. A. G.*

No. 7.]   HEADQUARTERS DISTRICT OF KENTUCKY,
LOUISVILLE, *July* 25, 1863.

By authority of the general commanding the department, the following general order is made:

1. It is ordered that no forage or other property belonging to loyal citizens in the State of Kentucky be seized or impressed except in cases of absolute necessity, and then only on the written authority from the headquarters of the twenty-third Army corps or from these headquarters.

2. Whenever it becomes necessary to seize or impress private property for military purposes, the property of sympathizers with the rebellion and of those opposed to furnishing any more men or any more money to maintain the Federal Government and suppress the rebellion will be first seized and impressed.

3. The negroes of loyal citizens will not be impressed on the public works and military roads unless absolutely necessary. The negroes of citizens who are for no more men and no more money to suppress the rebellion, and the supporters, aiders, and abettors of such, will be first impressed, and officers detailed for the purpose are required strictly to observe this order in the execution of their duties.

4. All horses of the enemy captured or subject to capture will be taken possession of by quartermasters and reported to Captain Jenkins, chief quartermaster, Louisville, who is ordered to allow loyal citizens to retain horses to supply the places of those stolen by the enemy ; but disloyal persons mentioned in paragraphs two and three, who encourage raids by the enemy, will not in any case be allowed to retain captured horses or horses justly subject to capture.

5. For all property seized or impressed proper and regular vouchers will be given, with indorsement as to the loyalty or disloyalty of the owners of the property.

By order of Brigadier General Boyle:

A. C. SEMPLE, *A. A. G.*

[General Orders, No. 23.]

HEADQUARTERS FIRST BRIGADE,
SECOND DIVISION, TWENTY-THIRD ARMY CORPS,
ROSSELLVILLE, KENTUCKY, *July* 30, 1863.

In order that the proclamation of the Governor and the laws of the State of Kentucky may be observed and enforced, post commandants and officers of this command will see that the following regulations are strictly complied with at the approaching State election :

None but loyal citizens will act as officers of the election.

No one will be allowed to offer himself as a candidate for office, or be voted for at said election, who is not in all things loyal to the State and Federal Government, and in favor of a vigorous prosecution of the war for the suppression of the rebellion.

The judges of election will allow no one to vote at said election unless he is known to them to be an undoubtedly loyal citizen, or unless he shall first take the oath required by the laws of the State of Kentucky.

No disloyal man will offer himself as a candidate, or attempt to vote, except for treasonable purposes; and all such efforts will be summarily suppressed by the military authorities.

All necessary protection will be supplied and guarantied at the polls to Union men by all the military force within this command.

By order of Brigadier General J. M. Shackleford, commanding :

J. E. HUFFMAN,
Assistant Adjutant General.

Oath to be taken at the Election.

I do solemnly swear that I have not been in the service of the so-called confederate States in either a civil or military capacity, or in the service of the so-called provisional government of Kentucky; that I have not given any aid, assistance or comfort to any person in arms against the United States; and that I have in all things demeaned myself as a loyal citizen since the beginning of the present rebellion; so help me God.

Colonel John W. Foster, of the sixty-fifth Indiana regiment, commanding post at Henderson, Kentucky, issued an order similar to the above order of General Shackleford.

[General Order.]

HEADQUARTERS UNITED STATES FORCES,
SMITHLAND, KENTUCKY, *July* 16, 1863.

The county court judges of the counties of Trigg, Caldwell, Lyon, Crittenden and Livingston, are hereby directed, in appointing judges and clerks for conducting the State elections in August next, to observe strictly the laws of Kentucky, which require that such judges and clerks shall be *unconditional Union men.*

Judges and clerks so appointed are hereby directed not to place the name of any person on the poll-books to be voted for at said election who is not a Union man, or who may be opposed to *furnishing men and money for a vigorous prosecution of the war* against the rebellion against the United States Government. The judges and clerks are further directed to permit no person to vote at said election without taking the oath required by the laws of Kentucky, unless said person so presenting himself to vote is personally known to the judges to be a Union man.

Any person violating this order will be regarded as an enemy to the Government of the United States, and will be arrested and punished accordingly.

By order of   THOMAS JOHNSON,
Lieutenant Colonel Commanding.

The oath prescribed by Lieutenant Colonel Johnson, to be taken by voters, is in substance similar to the oath attached to the proclamation of General Shackleford.

[Special Orders, No. 158.]

HEADQUARTERS SIXTEENTH ARMY CORPS,
MEMPHIS, TENNESSEE, *July,* 1863.

I. In so much of the State of Kentucky as is within the district of Columbus, it is ordered—

1. That no person be permitted to be a candidate for office who is not avowedly and unconditionally for the Union and the suppression of the rebellion.

2. That no person shall exercise the privilege of an elector and vote at said election who is not avowedly and unconditionally for the Union and the suppression of the rebellion.

3. The military authorities in said district of Columbus will see to it that this order be carried out. Judges of election will be governed by the principles herein set forth, and will demand evidence upon oaths in such cases as may be in doubt, and allow no person to exercise the franchise of voting who does not take the oath required.

By orders of Major General S. A. Hurlbut:

HENRY DINMORE,
Assistant Adjutant General.

[Orders.]

HEADQUARTERS DISTRICT OF COLUMBUS,
SIXTH DIVISION, SIXTEENTH ARMY CORPS,
COLUMBUS, KENTUCKY, *July* 15, 1863.

The above orders of the general commanding corps are communicated to the civil and military authorities for their information. Military officers making arrests for violation of these orders will be governed by the circular from office of Commissary General of Prison, dated Washington, May 11, 1863.

By order of Brigadier General Asboth.

T. H. HARRRIS.
Assistant Adjutant General.

[General Orders, No. 47.]

DISTRICT OF COLUMBUS,
HEADQUARTERS, SIXTH DIVISION,
SIXTEENTH ARMY CORPS,
COLUMBUS, Ky., July 00, 1860.

That no further doubt may exist as to the intent and meaning of Special Orders No. 159, dated Headquarters Sixteenth Army Corps, July 14, 1863, it is ordered that no person shall be permitted to be voted for, or be a candidate for office, who has been or is now under arrest or bonds, by property authority, for uttering disloyal language or sentiments.

County judges within this district are hereby ordered to appoint, as judges and clerks of the ensuing August election, only such persons as are avowedly and unconditionally for the Union and the suppression of the rebellion, and are further ordered to revoke and recall any appointment of judges and clerks already made, who are not such loyal persons.

Judges and clerks of elections are hereby ordered not to place the name of any person upon the poll-books, to be voted for at said election, who is not avowedly and unconditionally for the Union and the suppression of the rebellion, or may be opposed to furnishing men and money for the suppression of the rebellion.

The following oath is prescribed and will be administered by judges of elections to voters and to such candidates as reside within this district:

"I do solemnly swear that I have never entered the service of the so-called confederate States; that I have not been engaged in the service of the so-called 'provisional government of Kentucky,' either in a civil or military capacity; that I have never, either directly or indirectly, aided the rebellion against the Government of the United States or the State of Kentucky; that I am unconditionally for the Union and the suppression of the rebellion, and am willing to furnish men and money for the vigorous prosecution of the war against the rebellious league known as the 'confederate States;' so help me God."

Any voter, judge, or clerk of elections, or other persons, who may evade, neglect, or refuse compliance with the provisions of this order will be arrested and sent before a military commission as soon as the facts are substantiated.

By order of Brigadier General Asboth.

T. H. HARRIS,
Assistant Adjutant General.

On this order of General Asboth is the following indorsement:

I had the within order enforced in the counties of McCracken, Graves, Callaway, and Marshall.

J. S. MARTIN,
Colonel Commanding Post of Paducah.

No. 14.]   DEATSVILLE, NELSON COUNTY, KENTUCKY,
August 3, 1863.

I, Moses D. Leeson, captain commanding company B, fifth Indiana cavalry, hereby certify that under the orders and instructions of Lieutenant Colonel Thomas H. Butler, commanding fifth Indiana cavalry, I ordered the polls to be opened by the regularly appointed judges, sheriff, and clerk, namely, W. R. Livers, T. C. Warren, Thomas Cown, and R. E. Harrell, and permitted no other candidates' names to appear on the poll-books but the following: for Governor, Thomas E. Bramlette; for Lieutenant Governor, R. T. Jacob; for attorney general, John M. Harlan; for State treasurer, James Garrard; for auditor, W. T. Samuels; for register of land office, James A. Davidson; for superintendent of public instruction, Stevenson; for Congress, Aaron Harding; for the Legislature, Dr. W. Elliott; for county attorney, G. W. Hite; for county clerk, W. T. Spalding and William M. Powell.

MOSES D. LEESON,
Captain Commanding Company B, Fifth Indiana Cavalry.

No. 15.]

We, the undersigned, do hereby certify, as officers of Precinct No. 2, at Cloverport, Kentucky, that, after opening the polls, Captain Hernbook, by authority from General Shackleford, ordered us to strike off the entire Wickliffe

ticket, and also Milton Board's name, from the poll-book, which was accordingly done in obedience to said order.

WILLIAM B. JONES, }
WILLIAM S. ALLEN, } *Judges.*

Attest: J. C. Hest, *Clerk.*

J. R. Allen, Marshal.

FORKS OF ROUGH, *August* 3, 1863.

I do certify that at Rough Creek Spring precinct, District No. 4, there was a poll opened for C. A. Wickliffe and others forming a Democratic ticket, and for State officers; that I suppressed the same by order of General Shackleford, between seven and eight o'clock a. m.

WILLIAM BROWN,
Sergeant in Command.

[General Orders, No. 53.]

HEADQUARTERS MIDDLE DEPARTMENT,
EIGHTH ARMY CORPS,
BALTIMORE, MARYLAND, *October* 27, 1863.

It is known that there are many evil-disposed persons, now at large in the State of Maryland, who have been engaged in rebellion against the lawful Government, or have given aid and comfort or encouragement to others so engaged, or who do not recognize their allegiance to the United States, and who may avail themselves of the indulgence of the authority which tolerates their presence to embarrass the approaching election, or, through it, to foist onemies of the United States into power. It is therefore ordered,

1. That all provost marshals and other military officers do arrest all such persons found at, or hanging about, or approaching any poll or place of election on the 4th of November, 1863, and report such arrest to these headquarters.

2. That all provost marshals and other military officers commanding in Maryland shall support the judges of election on the 4th of November, 1863, in requiring an oath of allegiance to the United States, as the test of citizenship of any one whose vote may be challenged on the ground that he is not loyal, or does not admit his allegiance to the United States, which oath shall be in the following form and terms:

"I do solemnly swear that I will support, protect, and defend the Constitution and Government of the United States against all enemies, whether domestic or foreign; that I hereby pledge my allegiance, faith, and loyalty to the same, any ordinance, resolution, or law of any State convention or State Legislature to the contrary notwithstanding; that I will at all times yield a hearty and willing obedience to the said Constitution and Government; and will not, either directly or indirectly, do any act in hostility to the same, either by taking up arms against them, or aiding, abetting, or countenancing those in arms against them; that, without permission from the lawful authority, I will have no communication, direct or indirect, with the States in insurrection against the United States, or with either of them, or with any person or persons within said insurrectionary States; and that I will in all things deport myself as a good and loyal citizen of the United States. This I do in good faith, with full determination, pledge, and purpose to keep this, my sworn obligation, and without any mental reservation or evasion whatever."

3. Provost marshals and other military officers are directed to report to these headquarters any judge of an election who shall refuse his aid in carrying out this order, or who, on challenge of a vote being made on the ground of disloyalty or hostility to the Government, shall refuse to require the oath of allegiance from such voter.

By order of Major General Schenck:

W. H. CHESEBROUGH,
Lieutenant Colonel and Assistant Adjutant General.

WAR DEPARTMENT,
WASHINGTON, *November* 2, 1863.

SIR: Yours of the 31st ultimo was received yesterday about noon, and since then I have been giving most earnest attention to the subject-matter of it. At my call General Schenck has attended, and he assures me it is almost certain that violence will be used at some of the voting places on election day, unless prevented by his provost guards. He says that at some of those places the Union voters will not ttend at all, or run a ticket, unless they have some assurance of protection. This makes the Missouri case of my action, in regard to which you express your approval.

The remaining point of your letter is a protest against any person offering to vote being put to any test not found in the laws of Maryland. This brings us to a difference between Missouri and Maryland. With the same reason in both States, Missouri has, by law, provided a test for the voter with reference to the present rebellion, while Maryland has not. For example, General Trimble, captured fighting us at Gettysburg, is, without recanting his treason, a legal voter by the laws of Maryland. Even General Schenck's order admits him to vote, if he recants upon oath. I think that is cheap enough. My order in Missouri, which you approve, and General Schenck's order here, reach precisely the same end. Each assures the right of voting to all loyal men, and whether a man is loyal, each allows that man to fix by his own oath. Your suggestion that nearly all the candidates are loyal I do not think quite meets the case. In this struggle for the nation's life, I cannot so confidently rely on those whose election may have depended upon disloyal votes. Such men, when elected, may prove true, but such votes are given them in the expectation that they will prove false. Nor do I think that to keep the peace at the polls, and to prevent the persistently disloyal from voting, constitutes just cause of offense to Maryland. I think she has her own example for it. If I mistake not, it is precisely what General Dix did when your Excellency was elected Governor. I revoke the first of the three propositions in General Schenck's General Order No. 53, not that it is wrong in principle, but because the military being, of necessity, exclusive judges as to who shall be arrested, the provision is liable to abuse. For the revoked part I substitute the following:

That all provost marshals and other military officers do prevent all disturbance and violence at or about the polls, whether offered by such persons as above described, or by any other person or persons whatsoever.

The other two propositions of the order I allow to stand. General Schenck is fully determined, and has my strict order besides, that all loyal men may vote, and vote for whom they please.

Your obedient servant,

A. LINCOLN,
President of the United States.

His Excellency A. W. BRADFORD,
Governor of Maryland.

EXECUTIVE MANSION,
WASHINGTON, *January 20, 1864.*

Major General STEELE :

Sundry citizens of the State of Arkansas petition me that an election may be held in that State at which to elect a Governor ; that it be assumed at that election, and henceforward, that the constitution and laws of the State as before the rebellion are in full force, except that the constitution is so modified as to declare that there shall be neither slavery nor involuntary servitude, except in the punishment of crimes, whereof the party shall have been duly convicted ; that the General Assembly may make such provision for the freed people as shall recognize and declare their permanent freedom, and provide for their education, and which may yet be construed as a temporary arrangement suitable to their present condition as a laboring, landless, and homeless class ; that said election shall be held on the 28th of March, 1864, at all the usual places of the State, or all such as voters may attend for that purpose ; that the voters may attend at such place at eight o'clock in the morning of said day, may choose judges and clerks of election for that purpose ; that all persons qualified by said constitution and laws, and taking the oath presented in the President's proclamation of December 8, 1863, either before or at the election, and none others, may be voters ; that each set of judges and clerks may make returns directly to you, on or before the —— day of —— next ; that in all other respects said elections may be conducted according to said modified constitution and laws ; that, on receipt of said returns, when five thousand four hundred and six votes shall have been cast, you can receive said votes, and ascertain all who shall thereby appear to have been elected ; that on the —— day of —— next all persons appearing to have been elected, who shall appear before you at Little Rock, and take the oath, to be by you severally administered, to support the Constitution of th

United States and said modified constitution of the State of Arkansas ; and he by you declared qualified and to enter immediately upon the duties of the office to which they have been respectively elected.

You will please order an election to take place on the 28th of March, 1864, and returns to be made in fifteen days thereafter.

A. LINCOLN.

General Butler recently issued the following order :

(General Orders, No. 3.)

NORFOLK, VIRGINIA, *February 11, 1864.*

All places of public worship in Norfolk and Portsmouth are hereby placed under the control of the provost marshals of Norfolk and Portsmouth respectively, who shall see the pulpits properly filled by displacing, when necessary, the present incumbents, and substituting men of known loyalty and the same sectarian denomination, either military or civil, subject to the approval of the commanding general. They shall see that all churches are open freely to all officers and soldiers, white or colored, at the usual hour of worship, and at other times, if desired ; and they shall see that no insult or indignity be offered to them, either by word, look, or gesture, on the part of the congregation. The necessary expenses will be levied, as far as possible, in accordance with the previous usages or regulations of each congregation respectively.

No property shall be removed, either public or private, without permission from these headquarters.

By command of Brigadier General E. A. Will.

LOUISVILLE, *June 13, 1863.*

DEAR SIR : The undersigned, in behalf of many in all parts of this Commonwealth, believe it a political necessity to reorganize the Democratic party in the State, in association with those of the North who have stood by the Government and the Constitution throughout this deplorable civil war. They constitute the only political party of the North with whom any party South will have any affiliation, while a political association between the two sections of the country is indispensable to a restoration of the Union.

We cannot consent to the doctrine that the Constitution and laws are inadequate to the present emergency ; that the constitutional guarantees of liberty and property can be suspended by war.

Our fathers certainly did not intend that our Constitution should be a fair-weather document, to be laid away in a storm, or a fancy garment to be worn only in dry weather. On the contrary, it is in times like the present that constitutional restraints on the power of those in authority are needed.

We hold the Federal Government one of limited powers, that cannot be enlarged by the existence of civil commotion.

We hold the rights reserved to the States equally sacred with those granted to the United States. The Government has no more right to disregard the constitutions and laws of the States than the States have to disregard the Constitution and laws of the United States.

We hold that the Administration has committed grave errors in confiscation bills, lawless proclamations, and military orders setting aside constitutions and laws, and making arrests outside of military lines where there is no public danger to excuse it.

It is now obvious that the fixed purpose of the Administration is to arm the negroes of the South to make war upon the whites, and we hold it to be the duty of the people of Kentucky to enter against such a policy a solemn and most emphatic protest.

We hold as sacred and inalienable the right of free speech and a free press ; that the Government belongs to the people and not the people to the Government.

We hold this rebellion utterly unjustifiable in its inception, and a dissolution of the Union the greatest of calamities. We would see all just and constitutional means adopted to the suppression of the one and the restoration of the other.

Having observed your uniform and consistent course since the origin of our troubles, we believe you a faithful representative of our views, and urgently request that you

33

permit your name to be used as a Democratic candidate for Governor at the next ensuing election.

Yours respectfully,

W. F. BULLOCK,
ROBERT COCHRAN,
L. S. TRIMBLE,
THOMAS P. HUGHES,
R. C. PALMER,
ALFRED HERR,
J. P. CHAMBERS,
WILLIAM K. THOMAS,
WILLIAM G. REASOR,
ROBERT K. WHITE,
J. H. HARNEY,
WILLIAM KAYE,
N. WOLFE,
S. M. HALL,
JOHN HERR,
CHARLES L. HARRISON,
JOSHUA F. BULLITT,
GEORGE W. JOHNSTON,
ROBERT M. SMITH,
T. J. CONN,
W. A. DUDLEY,
W. P. SIMMONS,
JOHN T BRIDGES,
T. J. HALL,
SAMUEL N. HALL,
PHIL. TOMPPERT, Jr.,
JESSE F. HAMMON,
P. M. CAMPION,
W. H. BAILEY,
JACOB ABNY,
J. H. PRICE.

Hon. C. A. WICKLIFFE.

Extract from Statute of George II, chapter 30, [1735.]

An act for regulating the quartering of soldiers during the time of the elections of members to serve in Parliament.

Whereas, by the ancient common law of this land, all elections ought to be free; and whereas by an act passed in the third year of the reign of King Edward I, of famous memory, it is commanded upon great forfeiture that no man by force of arms nor by malice or menacing shall disturb any to make free election; and forasmuch as the freedom of elections of members to serve in Parliament is of the utmost consequence to the preservation of the rights and liberties of this kingdom; and whereas it hath been the usage and practice to cause any regiment, troop, or company, or any number of soldiers which hath been quartered in any city, borough, town, or place where any election of members to serve in Parliament hath been appointed to be made, to remove and continue out of the same during the time of such election, except in such particular cases as are hereinafter specified: To the end, therefore, that the said usage and practice may be settled and established for the future, *Be it enacted by the King's most excellent majesty, by and with the advice and consent of the lords spiritual and temporal and commons in Parliament assembled, and by the authority of the same,* That when and as often as any election of any peer or peers to represent the peers of Scotland in Parliament, or of any member or members to serve in Parliament shall be appointed to be made, the Secretary at War for the time being, or in case there shall be no Secretary at War, then such person who shall officiate in the place of the Secretary at War shall, and he is hereby required, at some convenient time before the day appointed for such election, to issue and send forth proper orders in writing for the removal of every such regiment, troop, or company, or other number of soldiers as shall be quartered or billeted in any such city, borough, town, or place where such election shall be appointed to be made, out of every such city, borough, town, or place, one day at the least before the day appointed for such election, to the distance of two or more miles from such city, borough, town, or place, and not to make any nearer approach to such city, borough, town, or

place as aforesaid until one day at the least after the poll to be taken at such election shall be ended, and the poll-books closed.

II. *And be it further enacted by the authority aforesaid,* That in the case the Secretary at War for the time being, or such person who shall officiate in the place of the Secretary at War, shall neglect or omit to issue or send forth such orders as aforesaid, according to the true intent and meaning of this act, and shall be thereof lawfully convicted upon any indictment to be preferred at the next assizes, or sessions of oyer and terminer, to be held for the county where such offense shall be committed, or on an information to be exhibited in the court of King's Bench, within six months after such offense committed, such Secretary at War, or person who shall officiate in the place of the Secretary at War, shall for such offense be discharged from their said respective offices and shall from thenceforth be utterly disabled, and made incapable to hold any office or employment, civil or military, in his Majesty's service.

An act to regulate elections, approved April 18, 1846.

"Sec. 33. No such election shall be appointed to be held, on any day on which the militia of that State shall be required to do military duty, nor shall the militia of this State be required to do military duty on any day on which any such election shall be appointed to be held."—*Nixon's Digest, Laws of New Jersey,* 1709-1855, p. 220.

Of the manner of conducting elections and returning votes.

"Sec. 1. No meeting for the election of national, State, district, county, city, or town officers, shall be held on a day upon which the militia of the Commonwealth are by law required to do military duty."—*General Statutes of Massachusetts,* 1860, chap. 7, p. 58.

Penal provisions and regulations affecting the purity of elections.

"Sec. 62. If any officer of the militia parades his men, or exercises any military command on a day of election of a public officer, as described in section sixty-three of chapter ten, and not thereby excepted, or except in time of war or public danger, he shall for each offense forfeit not less than ten nor more than three hundred dollars."—*Revised Statutes of Maine,* 1857, chap. 4, p. 84.

Penalties for the violation of election laws.

"Sec. 5. If any officer or other person shall call out or order any of the militia of this State to appear and exercise on any day during any election to be held by virtue of this chapter, or within five days previous thereto, except in cases of invasion or insurrection, he shall forfeit the sum of $500 for every such offense."—*Revised Statutes of New York, Banks & Brothers, Fifth Edition,* vol. 1, title 7, chap. 6, p. 448.

---

1. Of election by the citizens.

"110. No body of troops in the army of the United States shall be present, either armed or unarmed, at any place of election within this Commonwealth, during the time of such election: *Provided,* That nothing herein contained shall be so construed as to prevent an officer or soldier from exercising the right of suffrage in the election district to which he may belong if otherwise qualified according to law."—*Purdon's Digest; Brightly,* 1700-1861; *Laws of Pennsylvania,* p. 383.

www.ingramcontent.com/pod-product-compliance
Lightning Source LLC
Chambersburg PA
CBHW021450090426
42739CB00009B/1703